1

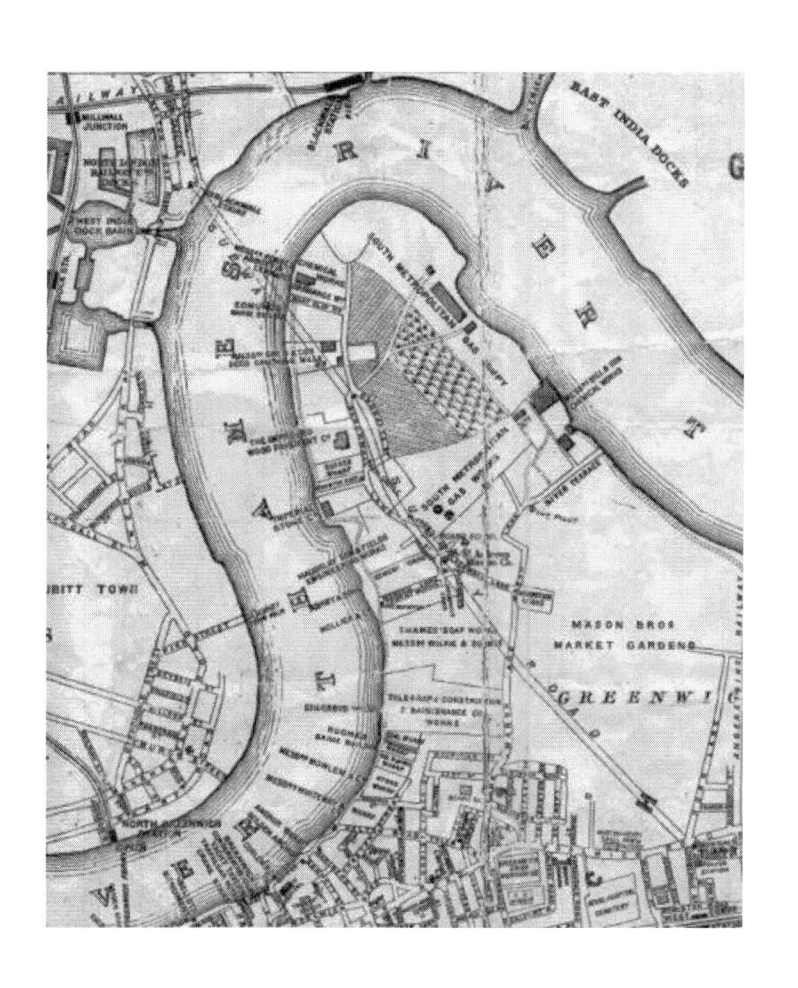

1

GREENWICH PENINSULA
GREENWICH MARSH

HISTORY OF AN INDUSTRIAL HEARTLAND

by

MARY MILLS

Copyright © Mary Mills
All rights reserved

South Met. East Greenwich Gas Works
1926

CONTENTS

Greenwich Marsh	6
Early industry on the marsh	13
Developers	21
The Telecommunications Revolution	32
This is all about coal tar	43
Engineers	53
Ship, Boat and barge building	65
Stone and bricks and cement	90
Coal fired power	99
Late 19th century industry	108
Houses large and small	116
Pubs	121
Docks, the River and railways	127
The Blackwall Tunnels	133
The 20th century	138
Development and the dome	150
Notes and references	162

5

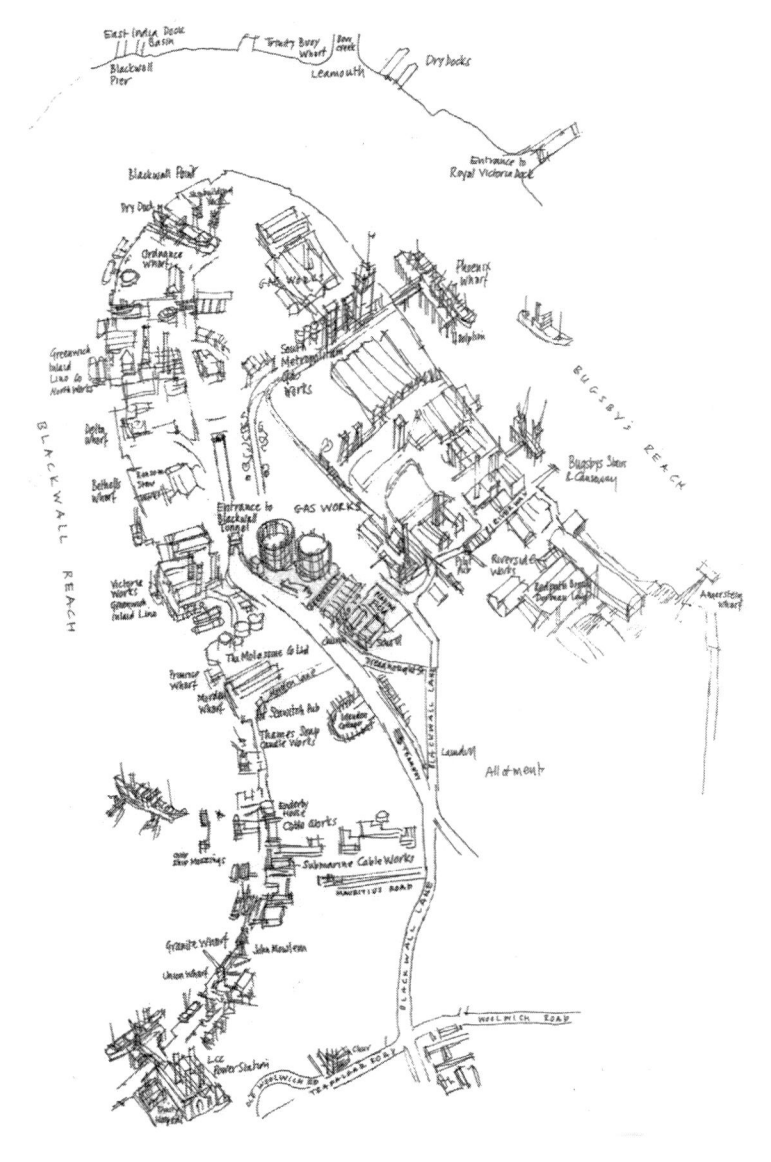

Some historical sites on Greenwich Peninsula 1880s-1980s.
Drawing by Peter Kent, with thanks

GREENWICH MARSH

The Greenwich Peninsula used to be called Greenwich Level - because a marsh is what it was - and what it still is, and a 'level' because it is flat. Before 1800 it was the most upriver point of the bleak and beautiful marshes on the south side of the Thames estuary - a place of *'wet land and dry water'*.

There was once a lot more water - a recent study of Greenwich in the Bronze Age found the remains of wooden track ways in Bellot Street 'to take advantage of good fishing'. It thought the Peninsula area itself was a series of marshy islands.

The area that the marsh covered is easily defined. The loops of the Thames as it winds between London and its estuary are very clear on maps and, down River of Greenwich, 'proper', it loops round a finger of land. The southern boundary is neatly defined by Woolwich Road the main road between Greenwich and Woolwich. An eastern land boundary is formed by Peartree Way, but parallel to that is older Horn Lane, itself parallel to a 16th century flood barrier called Lambarde's Wall and the Greenwich Parish boundary.

The most northerly point of the Peninsula was once known as Lea Ness – the 'nose' of land facing Bow Creek. More recently this northerly point has been known as 'Blackwall Point,' Black Wall being the sea 'wall' on the eastern side of the Isle of Dogs. Now it is the site of the Dome.

Were the Romans here? I used to meet people working nearby who claimed to have picked up Roman relics when the Dome was being built but none of them were archaeologists and no-one said who had identified them as Roman. My guess is that the Romans, in four or so centuries, got everywhere.

First excavation of 12th Century tide mill on what was Granite Wharf

From the 10th century until 1414 the area was owned by St.Peter's Abbey in Ghent. In 2008 an early medieval tide mill was discovered on the site of what has since become Riverside Gardens – previously Granite Wharf. It is thought that this belonged to the Abbey and that Ballast Quay was their wharf. Further toward Greenwich on Highbridge was the Abbey's courthouse, upmarket accommodation and offices, which was demolished only in the 1690s.

Through the mediaeval period Greenwich marsh was in 'The Manor of Old Court'. Once the Tudor Court had moved to Greenwich the land and manorial rights were owned by a series of grandees. By the 16th century most of it was owned by the Crown and within the next hundred years, with some small exceptions, it had passed into the hands of charities, which leased land out to whoever wanted to use it. They are the bodies who have shaped the present.

Until the late 19th century Greenwich was part of the County of Kent and its proximity to the capital helped determine how the land was used.

THE MARSH SINCE 1315

We can only guess what marsh was like a thousand years ago, or what it would be now, without constant maintenance. In 1315 a Commission was set up to look after the River wall and ditches. From the early 17th century management was undertaken by the Court of Sewers and the minutes of their meetings, dating from 1625, are held in the London Metropolitan Archive. The Court was made up of landowners and their tenants and administered a programme of ditches to be cleaned and brambles to be cut back. A bailiff was employed to get the work done and the Wallscot tax paid for it. The Court continued for over 200 years until its duties were taken over by Greenwich Board of Works and later the London County Council.

On 17th century maps a lane is shown running through the marsh. It left the Woolwich Road at the Ship and Billet pub (currently called The Duchess Bar). Marsh Lane went north from the Woolwich Road and then divided - one arm going east and the other straight ahead. These lanes are still there known as Blackwall Lane while the easterly arm has more recently been known as Riverway, albeit now cut off from the River following a 1990s re-design by the New Millennium Experience Company.

The marsh was made up of fields - the boundaries of many of them made up the areas of the later factories, and today many blocks of flats are on the same footprint – although sadly many are not. Their names have now entirely disappeared - among them were The Pitts, Balsopps, Goose Marsh and Cat's Brains. We can only speculate on why they were given these names.

By 1625 the most important work had been done towards establishing a drainage system in order to allow the land to be used for farming and similar pursuits. Bendish Sluice emerged by Enderby's Wharf; Arnold's Sluice entered the Thames to the north east of Blackwall Point; King's Sluice was near Horn Lane and there was another to the south west of Blackwall Point. These sluices were a major civil engineering project carried out by experts. They may have been contracted by the Commissioners to a Jacobus Acontyus, who had left Italy because of his religious views and in 1566 to John Baptista Castillion, one of Queen Elizabeth's inner household. Without them the Peninsula would not exist in the form it does today.

THE SEA WALL

The other major work done before records began was the building of the sea wall. It was called the 'sea wall' not the 'River wall' because of the power of the tidal river and the strength needed to hold it back. So important was - and is - care and maintenance of the wall that local taxes were called the 'wallscot'.

Before 1625, the River broke its banks and the result was 'Horseshoe Breach', which was never repaired and is still there today. There was a constant sense of urgency in case a storm should lead to another such disaster. A few dangerously high tides would quickly lead to calls for something to be done.

A number of well-known engineers worked on the wall. In the late 1820s a serious problem arose on the west bank. The top civil engineers of the day were asked for their opinions. Thomas Telford thought the problems were caused by the large number of ships using the recently opened West India Docks. The Court of Sewers had great difficulty in raising the money to pay him even though an arrangement had been made with the wealthy charity, Morden College, to buy some of the land affected. They later refused to pay John Rennie, Jnr., also brought in as a consultant, and his arrogant complaint that 'Nothing annoys me so much as disputes about payments' did nothing to improve relationships. Telford eventually undertook the job and his work lies somewhere on the west bank at the northern end of the Peninsula.

There were other problems with the sea and the riverbank. For instance, throughout the 19th century the Court of Sewers accused the lightermen who worked for Trinity House and the

Corporation of the City of London of removing stone from the sea wall to use as ballast – something always denied by the authorities concerned. Conversely in 1843 it was proposed to dump mud, excavated from the West India Dock on the wall itself. As late as 1890 a firm was operating a 'mud shute' there.

The wall has been continuously rebuilt throughout its existence and a great deal more recently. It is in need of constant care

EARLY BUILDINGS

Before 1800 little was built on the marsh beyond a few sheds and barns. No one lived there and for many years there were gates with a gatekeeper to stop casual visitors. A watch house, or perhaps a building connected with River defences, was built in the middle of the marsh. There has been speculation about some sort of Tudor defence structure, perhaps a 'boom' built across the River at Blackwall. At one time a watchman was employed – and in any case a depot of some sort would have been needed by the marsh bailiff and his staff, to keep tools and maybe for shelter and break periods.

The first major building was probably the Gunpowder Depot (of which more later) and the Court of Sewers complained bitterly about the behaviour of soldiers posted there. Even after 1800 few people lived in the area apart from the little community around The Pilot, which grew up after 1802.

In the south part of the marsh, in the area adjacent to the Woolwich Road, housing of a good standard was provided under the supervision of Morden College from the 1840s and this area is still flourishing. In the late 19th century some factories provided homes for their workers. Gradually a community of cottages and tenements grew up. Most of the people who lived there had little choice but to put up with damp conditions in what was still a down-market area.

Gradually amenities were built - a church, mission halls, shops, more pubs, schools, 'dining rooms', and so on. Much of this community was destroyed by the London County Council and the local authority in the 1960s and 1970s because it was thought people should not live in such a heavily industrialised marshland area. By 1990 only the cottages by the Pilot remained plus two houses in Blackwall Lane near Ordnance Draw Dock.

OWNERSHIP OF THE MARSH

After 1700, although some plots of land were in private hands, most of the area was owned by large charities. They could afford to take a long term and detached view and, as we shall see, they were very important in determining how the marsh developed.

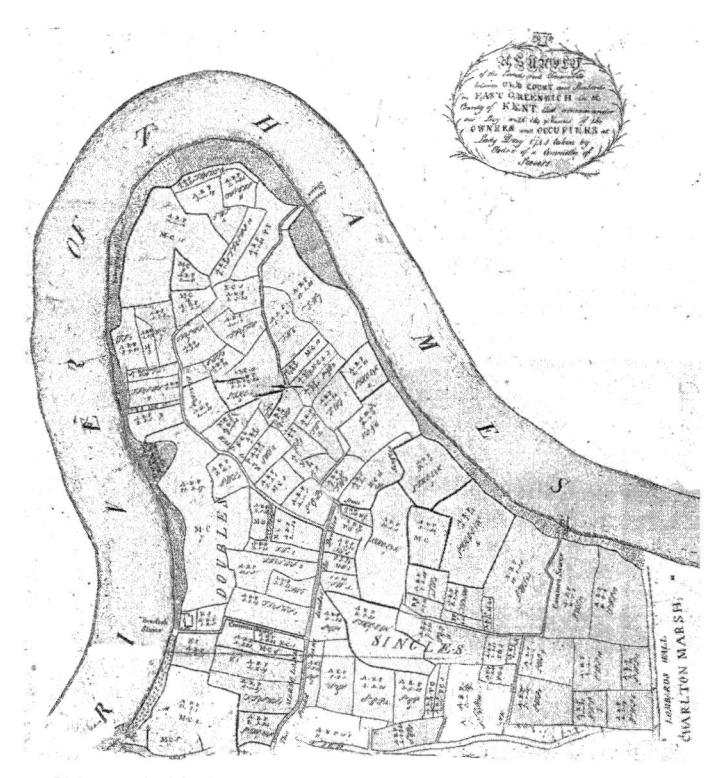

Skinner 1746 plan - each plot is coded for ownership, and use (usually by a leaseholder)

They were:

The Boreman Charity: At the Restoration of Charles II, after the English Civil War and the Commonwealth, a large parcel of land was granted to a Sir William Boreman by the King. Some of it was sold by his widow but the remainder went to help pay for a charity school which Boreman had founded in Greenwich. This charity was, and is still, administered by the Worshipful Company of Drapers. Their lands were sold in the 1870s - but management decisions taken by them still have an effect.

Trinity Hospital (Norfolk College): On the Greenwich riverfront, near the London Underground Power Station, is a little 'Strawberry Hill Gothic' almshouse. This is another charity, often known as 'Trinity Hospital', which dates from 1613, and is administered by the Worshipful Company of Mercers. Part of the marsh was owned by them until the early 1880s.

The Poor of Farningham: a few fields were administered for the benefit of poor people in the parish of Farningham in Kent. This was land left by a benefactor from the Roper family.

Hatcliffe's Charity.: land was owned by Hatcliffe's Charity - whose almshouse still stands in Tuskar Street in Greenwich and resulted from a Jacobean bequest.

MORDEN COLLEGE

Morden College: The land which Boreman's widow sold in 1698 was bought by a merchant, Sir John Morden. He used it to endow Morden College one of the most important, but least known, institutions in Greenwich. They have been a major influence in the history of Greenwich marsh and its industries.

John Roque's map of London, published in 1744, shows Greenwich Marsh and Blackwall Lane. South of it is the open space of Blackheath and on the far side is a large square building built around a quadrangle and marked 'Morden College'. These buildings, shown on the 19th century map, are just the same today. So many modern institutional buildings are in the Wren style that it is sometimes difficult to take in that sometimes you are looking at the real thing. The only change is that the 'decayed Turkey merchants', for whom it was set up, are now in short supply and the charity houses, in accordance with its charter, those who have fallen on hard times in old age.

Sir John Morden died in 1708. In his will he laid down that the College was to be managed by nominees of the Turkey Company, if this failed the East India Company, and on their demise the Court of Aldermen of the Corporation of the City of London. This succession has duly proceeded. Should they be abolished Sir John's requirement was that future management should be by 'seven discreet and grave Gentlemen of Kent'.

Throughout the 19th century the Chairmen of Morden College's trustees were bankers, some were members of the Lubbock family, based in Farnborough, Kent. The trustees did, and do, the best they could to maximise land values for the good of the charity with which they were entrusted.

Much of the pattern of Greenwich marsh's future was shaped by Morden College, and its surveyors. They were concerned with building standards and the type of activity to be allowed on their sites. For a period in the 19th century the same man, George Smith, held the position of surveyor to both Morden College and the Mercers' Company and, as will be seen, he played a key role in the marsh's development.

Much of the information in this book has been gleaned from Morden College's wonderful archive – for which I would like to thank them.

THE NATURAL WORLD

Greenwich Marsh has not been 'natural' for many hundreds of years, probably longer. It became man-made when the River was kept out of it and the land has been managed from the time it was reclaimed from the River. When human economic activity in this area moved away from farming into what we think f as industry, then factories were built on the marsh to replace agriculture.

The land has been used for the economic benefit of those who did not live there. The area has been shaped by people, many of whom were bankers in the City of London and who had probably never seen it.

Black poplar on Greenwich Marsh before industry came

EARLY INDUSTRY ON THE MARSH

Industry came surprisingly slowly to Greenwich Marsh – despite the fact that Greenwich itself was a manufacturing town from at least Tudor times.

The marsh is said to have been used for 'rural industry'. This indicates commercial activity which is clearly different to subsistence farming. Morden College records show that, although some fields were let to the tenants of surrounding farms who grazed cattle and sheep on the marsh, some tenants were 'butchers' who kept stock there on a short-term basis before sending it to market. Growing reeds and willow as cash crops was a typical commercial use and at least one leaseholder was a 'basket maker' using these plants as their raw material. Marshlands have a particular economy of their own and no doubt there were eel traps and wild fowling alongside grazing and reed beds.

The River provided the main means of transport. 'Watermen' used the marshland and there is a record of one being evicted from his landing place for unknown reasons in 1694.

Throughout the early 19th century some fields were let to a Mr.Wheatley, who ran a local horse omnibus service – a reminder that the factories described were surrounded by meadows used for grazing. Wheatley had once run a major network of routes but by the 1860s was reduced to plying between the local railway stations. Nevertheless there were still horses to feed and throughout the 19th century Wheatley could be found renting meadows from Morden College. Much of the central area of the marsh retained a rural character into the early 20th century. There is even a photograph from the 1920s of a small haystack in Blackwall Lane.

There is no evidence of any housing on the marsh until the early 19th century. There are occasional hints of what appear to be hideouts by those seeking to evade the public view and presumably they were dealt with by the Marsh Bailiff in due course.

THE GOVERNMENT GUNPOWDER MAGAZINE

The location of the Tudor Palace and court in Greenwich in the early 16th century had led to the setting up of two Royal Dockyards and the establishment of arms manufacture locally and this accelerated after the English Civil War. Greenwich armour was famous in the 16th century and the armoury mill, on the Lewisham borders, later produced small arms. In the 19th century it moved to Enfield. The Royal Arsenal itself had some origins which could be traced to the 'Great Barn' on the Palace site.

The Government Gunpowder Magazine
With thanks to the Martin Collection

At the end of the 17th century a large building, by any definition 'industrial', was established on the west bank of the Marsh – on the area now known as Enderby Wharf. This was a Crown establishment and it marks a change in the way the Marsh was exploited.

A complementary activity to armaments manufacture was the storage and distribution of gunpowder. This had been stored in the Tower of London but in 1694 the Principal Officers advised the Treasury that they needed funding for a new 'Powderhouse' where gunpowder could be delivered by the manufacturers, then tested and distributed as required. What was needed was a remote riverside site near London. They chose a site on the West Bank of the marsh - near where Enderby House stands today.

The 'Royal Magazine' consisted of a large 'proof house' where the gunpowder was tested for quality. This was large, featureless, windowless and square. There were two wings, one with a chimney and there was a spire on the roof for venting the controlled explosions during testing. There was a large double wharf known as 'the bridge' with two pairs of gates.

The powder was made in privately owned mills throughout the south east of England, in the Lea Valley at Sewardstone and Enfield, on the Thames at Bedfont, south of London at Chilworth, and Wimbledon, and down river at Faversham. It was transported to Greenwich by water and, once tested; it was sent to naval depots as well as to garrisons and naval bases as far away as Jamaica and Nova Scotia.

Thousands of barrels of explosives passed through the depot every year. As well as the skilled workers who tested the powder there was an army of clerks. These workers were 'settled' with a permanent job in the government service. Two 'proofmasters' were in charge of the depot and there was a storekeeper. In 1754, for example, this was Robert Furnis, who lived in a single storey building on site.

LOCAL OBJECTIONS TO GUNPOWDER

Not surprisingly Greenwich residents did not appreciate the presence of this large store of explosives on their doorsteps. In 1718 and again in 1750 they petitioned Parliament to have it removed.

> "Reason for removing the Magazine of Gunpowder at Greenwich to some more convenient place and further Distance from the said Town and the Cities of London and Westminster.
> The apparent Danger the said Magazine is exposed to, of being blown up by Treachery, lightning and other Accidents, arising from its present defenceless Situation and ruinous condition, and the extensive and scarce repairable Damage with which the Explosion of perhaps 6 or 8,000 barrels of powder must be attended, cannot but cause terrible apprehensions to all who seriously consider it.

Eventually, Government inspectors decided that the Greenwich Depot did indeed present a risk and recommended that it should be moved to Purfleet. The last powder was delivered in 1768 and the depot closed soon after. The entire workforce went to Purfleet except for a Robert Dyer, who was old and ill and so retired with a pension

What happened to the buildings after they were closed? The inspectors had said that they were 'improperly and dangerously situated' and 'utterly incapable of being effectually repaired' and they appear to have been demolished in 1770. Thirty years later the site was apparently sold, to Henry Vansittart, a Vice-Admiral. It continued to be described as 'Crown Lands' in official documents until at least 1808.

There was an echo of the public disquiet about the works in 1815, when a private gunpowder magazine was planned in Charlton. A petition was quickly put together pointing out the fears that local people had had about the old magazine.

In 1846 a pub in Eastney Street was burnt to the ground. It was a dreadful fire and a bedridden old lady was only rescued through the 'bold daring of a young sailor.' The pub's name was the 'Royal Magazine', evidence that the Gunpowder Depot was remembered, if only by Greenwich drinkers.

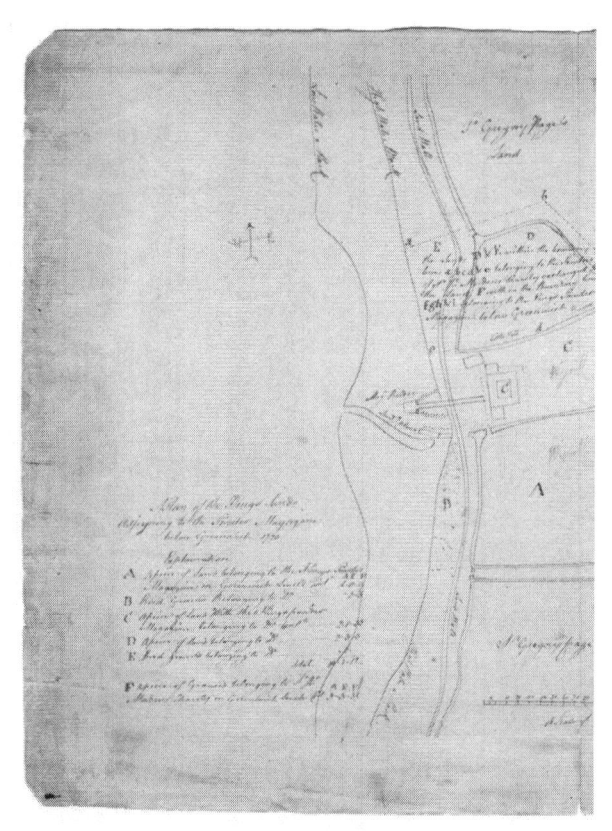

Plan of the Government Gunpowder Magazine
(Martin Collection with thanks)

AN EARLY CHEMICAL INDUSTRY

As the 18th century progressed there were signs of the arrival of new industries in the area around the site of the gunpowder depot. There may have been a bleach works before 1770 at Dog Kennel Field, where there was a 'Whiters House and Garden'. This probably meant it was used for the bleaching of paper or cloth. If so it was in effect the first commercial industrial premises on the marsh. Seventy years later a 'bleaching house' was apparently near the riverside on Bendish Marsh

Traditional bleaching methods needed space and water. There were flourishing bleach fields close by Greenwich, north of the Thames in the Lea Valley and east along the Darenth Valley. Samuel Parkes, a writer on chemistry who knew London well, commented in 1839 that from around 1750 sulphuric acid began to be used in bleaching processes. In this context it should be noted that there may also have been a vitriol - i.e. sulphuric acid - factory established nearby owned by a Lewis Price.

It might be conjectured that the site on the Peninsula riverside was connected to a possible copperas works, a process involving producing liquor from pyrites which was often associated with vitriol manufacture. Such a works was then in use on the Greenwich side of Deptford Creek possibly by a George Moore. It may not be a co-incidence that a George Moore also leased fields in this area of the Peninsula.

These early industrial sites were in the area now known as Enderby Wharf, soon to be developed further by the Enderby family

BUGSBY AND THE GIBBETS

Between east and west sides of the Peninsula a long stretch of river bank was used for a gruesome spectacle. This was the display of the rotting bodies of men executed, normally for piracy, as a deterrent to others, particularly passing sailors

The Marsh from the River - note the gibbet

The 'upper' gibbet stood on the River edge near Blackwall Point on the tip of the Peninsula and a 'lower' gibbet was near Bugsby's Hole, and the earliest reference to it is in 1735, when the body of Thomas Williams the pirate was hung there after his death at Execution Dock in Wapping. Williams had been convicted at a specially convened Admiralty Court for "*running away with the ship Buxton Snow, late Captain Beard, bound from Bristol to the Island of Malemba Angola in Africa, and selling the Ship; and also the Murder of the said Captain Beard, by cutting his Throat with an axe*".

The report of Williams' gibbeting is one of the first references to Bugsby – today we have Bugsby's Reach on the River and Bugsby's Way on the land. But Bugsby him (or her) self had always appeared elusive.

THE PILOT

The Pilot Inn now stands in a sort of courtyard called 'Riverway'. Until 2000 this was a road which led to the river and a long causeway, which was removed by the builders of the Millennium Dome. A 'hole' in the River is a traditional term meaning 'an anchorage'. Earlier this stretch of the River was called Cockle's Reach or Podd's Elms Reach. There have been a number of theories as to Bugsby's identity. Was he a market gardener? Or was he a robber hiding out in the osier beds? There is no record of either. Round the world there are other 'Bugsby's Holes' – one as near as Sheerness but another as far away as St. Helena. One possible solution has come from the US where a Mr. Bugby has good evidence of ancestors in this area.

DEVELOPMENT AT BUGSBY'S HOLE

In 1802 a large tide mill was built on the riverside near the site of 'The Jetty' today. Most of what we know about the mills comes from Mathematics Professor Olinthus Gregory. He visited the mill while it was under construction. And spoke at length to the site foreman, a Mr. Dryden who was, incidentally, very critical of the plans. It was built by the specialist millwrights Lloyd and Ostell based near Blackfriars Bridge.

The developer of the mill was a soap maker, George Russell, who had a soap works at Old Barge House, by Blackfriars Bridge. In his old age, Russell had bought land on Greenwich Marsh but died before the mill was completed. Initially his workmen made bricks there. This dirty, smelly, activity began to worry the marsh bailiff, Philip Sharpe. One day in April 1796, he walked down to the site and met Thomas Taylor. An argument developed. Taylor said 'Damn your eyes Mr Sharpe, if you come here I will polish your teeth and stop your eyes with mud, Sir!' He followed this up by ordering John Bicknell, who was standing nearby, to push Sharpe off the River wall. Bicknell, a young lad who would later be the Greenwich Vestry Clerk, did as he was told.

Soon after, Mr. Russell applied for official permission to build a wharf and causeway into the River. A William Johnson also applied for permission to cut the bank and erect a flour mill. Johnson came from Liverpool but was living in Bromley, Kent, with a young family.

On the wall of The Pilot is a plaque to 'New East Greenwich 1802' (pictured above) and it maybe that Russell intended to build a new industrial village here. The plans included the row of cottages and The Pilot as well as a 'big house' on the riverside – called East Lodge. The cottages are generally known as Ceylon Place, a name which can be explained by national events. In 1802, the year of the construction of the cottages, Ceylon was ceded to the British Crown as part of the Treaty of Amiens.

A document of 1842 refers to a lease on the site between the Rt. Hon. John Earl of Chatham, the Rt. Hon. William Pitt, the Rt. Hon. Crags and Lord Eliot with the Hon. John Eliot. What did this group of elite politicians have to do with the mill?

There may also be another link to William Pitt – and that is The Pilot itself. At a celebratory dinner for the Treaty of Amiens a song was written 'here's to the Pilot that Weathered the storm'. The pilot in the song is Prime Minister William Pitt.

THE REALLY REALLY IMPORTANT ACCIDENT

We now encounter a drama which was to shake the development of the steam engine and to damage the reputation of one of our most important engineers. The many references to it in histories of steam ascribe its site to anywhere between Rotherhithe and Woolwich – but it happened here in East Greenwich at the end of Marsh Lane, near The Pilot.

The use of high pressure steam had been thought dangerous and difficult to use but was developed by the Cornish engineer, Richard Trevithick. George Russell ordered an 8 horse power high pressure engine from Trevithick to be used during construction work of the mill.

As building work progressed the steam engine began to give some concern. The fire was in direct contact with the cast iron boiler which overheated on 4th September. The engine was the responsibility of an, unnamed, apprentice. On the following Thursday, 8th September, this boy was asked to catch eels from under the foundations of the building. Before he went he wedged a piece of timber at the top of the safety value and then bent it down so that it could not rise. The result was inevitable. The boiler burst 'with an explosion as sudden and as dreadful as a powder mill'. One piece an inch thick and weighing 5 cwt was thrown 125 yards in the air and 'landing on the ground made a hole eighteen inches deep'.

Three men were killed instantly, and three more were injured. One worker went deaf but the eel catching boy fully recovered. Another worker, Thomas Nailor, had been showered with boiling water and a wherry was called and he was taken to St.Thomas Hospital – then still on its old site in the Borough – but despite the work of Mr. Bingham, the surgeon, he died three days later.

The newspapers were quick to report the accident although the story was given to them by those who did not wish Trevithick well. He said 'Boulton and Watt are about to do me every injury in their power for they have done the best to report the explosion both in the newspapers and in private letters very different to what it really was'. He made some changes to the design of his boilers and in future his boilers had more than one safety vent.

Work continued on construction. The mill was finished and began work. Johnson lived in the Mill House until 1807, when he went off to the Maldon area. Soon there was to be more upheaval at the newly constructed mill. It was, to put it shortly, falling down.

TROUBLE AT THE MILL

Following Russell's death in 1804 the estate went into Chancery and was administered on their behalf by Sharpe and Handasyde. They called in Bermondsey based engineer Brian Donkin to give an opinion on the state of the mill. Only seven years old it was sinking, causing the walls to twist. A solution would need extensive and expensive engineering work, including changes to the mill ponds and the riverside. Donkin employed his friend John Hall from Dartford to do the work. This was a massive and major project and it was accompanied by constant complaints from

Sharp and the other executors to keep costs down and to work faster. In 1812 Sharp went bankrupt and Handasyde denied having had any money belonging to the estate. Hall consulted his solicitor and in 1813 a court found Handasyde was liable for the debt.

By around 1820 there were thus two industrial sites developed on the Peninsula. On the east side the site of the old gunpowder depot had been through several uses and would soon be, as well will, see a rope and then a cable works. On the east bank was a mill and a small settlement of housing.

Richard Trevithick

DEVELOPERS

Early industrial development on both east and west bank sites on the Peninsula was on limited sites. Landowners, many of them charities, began to evaluate the future of their holdings. These bodies were governed by trustees required to maximise their income for the benefit of the charitable institutions – and responsible development of their land was well within their remit.

The charity with the largest holding was, and still is, Morden College and in 1838 they asked their then surveyor, George Smith, to evaluate their land holdings on Greenwich marsh.

Morden College land lies largely along the west bank of the Peninsula from Ballast Quay at East Greenwich to what was Ordnance Wharf adjacent to where the Dome now stands. In this chain of sites there is one large exception in other ownership. That is the site of the old Government gunpowder works' which was soon to be taken over by one of the most revolutionary industries on the Peninsula.

In time Morden College adopted a policy of parcelling up land, usually based on old field sites, and leasing them to a principal developer with a remit to sub-let to other industries with good quality buildings. The whole process was to be monitored by the College Surveyor. Within 20 years there was a multiplicity of works on their sites with many different functions in a process which continued up to the 1990s and still to some extent influences these sites today

Other charities' landholdings were not so large although they too began to develop, as did some of the private individual owners.

On the west bank, development continued around the mill site but most of the west and the central area remained untouched until the 1880s, and then the main incomer was the huge works of the South Metropolitan Gas Company.

Infrastructure also remained largely untouched through the 19th century with works served by river traffic. Some plans were made, and one railway built but it was not until the end of the 19th century that things began to change with the building of the Blackwall Tunnel and installation of trams but it was the end of the 20th century before rail was introduced.

Apart from the cottages around the mill housing built was close enough to East Greenwich to be integrated into it. Gradually more workplace housing was developed but – apart from pubs – it was a long time before shops and a church arrived around Blackwall Lane, all to be removed by slum clearance in the 1960s

View upriver 1662

MORDEN COLLEGE AND EARLY DEVELOPMENT

The landholdings of Morden College on the Peninsula begin at Ballast Quay and begin at the corner of Pelton Road where it meets the riverside. It appears that a stile or gate there marked the boundary and is described in 1792 as a 'wicket with lock and key' and which is shown on an 18th century print.

The wharf has been known as 'Ballast Quay' since at least the 17th century and is marked as such on Travers' map of 1695. The name seems to refer to the transfer of ballast, perhaps gravel or chalk, into vessels. Such ballast was commonly put into collier ships which brought coal to London from north-eastern ports and which needed a return load. Morden College owned many pits from which gravel or chalk could be extracted in Blackheath and in Chiselhurst, and close by the site which is now Maze Hill Station.

From 1704 a grand building on the site of Greenwich Power Station was concerned with a complex of warehousing on Ballast Quay owned by Ambrose Crowley and his family. This was warehousing for his iron founding business based on the Tyne.

By 1792 Anchor Iron Wharf had been built out into the River. There was the Green Man Pub and sluices on the line of what would become Pelton Road. The area was later leased by Morden College to 'Millington' – Crowley's Manager and associate.

In 1818 Morden College's then Surveyor, Reginald Biggs, undertook a survey and drew a plan of the Quay, which shows little more than a line of trees and some sluices. It was nevertheless the start of a great deal of work here. In 1829 there was a proposal for 'a new wharf and improvements' roughly on the line of the current houses. In 1838 another survey by Biggs shows the Union Tavern - now the Cutty Sark Pub - and the distinctive line of the houses.

This is clearly the earliest attempt at development of the area, albeit for housing and a pub.

From 1839 Morden College's surveyor was George Smith. He was an architect who had already been responsible for some important buildings in Greenwich. He was also Surveyor to the Cator Estate in Blackheath, and would soon be appointed as architect to the Greenwich Railway. Crucially he was also Surveyor to the Mercers' Company, managing their land holdings on Greenwich Marsh for the Trinity Hospital. Thus he represented the two largest landholders and he held these key positions over the next fifty years.

Smith's work with Morden College had a very clear pattern. Sites were handed over to key tenants who 'improved' them and then sub-let to industrial users, all of whom had to be approved by Morden College. Buildings to be erected were expected to be of a high standard, and had to be approved by Smith. There was usually a requirement for housing to be designed by Smith, and the work subjected to his approval. One of the earliest sites to be developed under Smith's guidance was Dog Kennel Field. The developer was Coles Child who was a coal trader.

COLES CHILD

William Coles Child's family business, of coal, iron, cement and lime, was based on the Lambeth riverside, at Belvedere Wharf, near today's South Bank Centre. The business was typical of many that were beginning to take advantage of the expansion in canals, railways, and industry generally. Coles Child was only in his late teens when he took on the family business after his father's death. Five years later he approached Morden College for the tenancy of a portion of the 'Great Meadow', which stretched, between the River, the Enderby works and what is now Pelton Road. He wanted to 'form wharves, and erect manufactories thereon'.

Morden College told Child that in return for a lease at East Greenwich he would be expected to spend at least £3,000 on 'substantial buildings, a road, an embankment, and drainage', making it quite clear that what was expected was an 'advantageous development'. As negotiations proceeded they intimated that they also expected housing to be built there. Within a few months Child had offered to spend £4,000 on embankments and buildings and an agreement was made on Morden College's terms. His sites were on what had been the Great Meadow and Dog Kennel Field.

Morden College's archives contain abundant material about Coles Child' and what sometimes seems to have been his nuisance value. The Minutes of the Trustees record their refusals to his frequent written requests, together with reports from Smith. The quality of the coal that he supplied to the College was a constant cause of complaint. It is very likely, however, that he was personally known to some of the trustees - in particular the Chairman Sir John

William Lubbock, and his son and successor, Sir John Lubbock. They were bankers with strong personal links to the scientific community.

The Lubbock home and estates were at High Elms, Farnborough, on the outskirts of Bromley, Kent. They were thus near neighbours of Coles Child who, in 1846, bought the old Bishops' Palace in Bromley, now Bromley Civic Centre. Bromley Palace is almost, but not quite, as grand as it sounds, and Child's life style would have been eclipsed by the Lubbocks at High Elms. It has been speculated that some of his wealth came from selling his Belvedere Road wharf to the Charing Cross Railway in 1863. He was involved with many railway companies in Kent and sat on their boards while deriving profits from commodity sales to them.

Railways are great consumers of coal and coke and a good investment for someone whose money came from the haulage of bricks and coal. Coles Child seems to have set himself to transform the market town of Bromley by his intervention in public affairs and his specially grown prize winning hops. He also intervened in Greenwich politics. His grave is the most prominent in Bromley churchyard.

COAL

Industrial development on the Greenwich riverside quickly went ahead. The River wall was rebuilt and by 1840 Coles Child had erected limekilns and coke ovens. Gravel from Morden College sites at Blackheath Point was used for these projects. He also considered building a tramway along the Willow Dyke, already taking shape as Pelton Road.

In the 1840s haulage companies, which today use lorries, mainly used sailing barges and they also diversified into making the bricks and lime that they carried routinely for others. It is still easy to see the scars of the chalk pits down river at Northfleet and Grays and around the Medway. Many cement manufacturers began their profession as lime burners. Coal was brought from north east ports by fleets of colliers which often carried a cargo of lime on their return trip. It is this trade which Coles Child served. In the 18th century lime burning had been an important industry in the Greenwich area, often on sites owned by Morden College to the east of Greenwich South Street and Lewisham Road. Many of these sites were used for residential development in the late 18th and early 19th centuries. Pits from which chalk and gravel for ballast were dug could be found between Greenwich and Woolwich and at the back of what is now Maze Hill Station and at Charlton Football Ground.

In 1840 Child was 'pleased to announce' his facilities in the Kentish Mercury. Coals and coke could be supplied 'at a considerable reduction in price because of the facilities possessed by no other house' for 'purchase of coals at the pit's mouth'. In Greenwich coal could be loaded directly from the hold of the ship into the wagons, thus 'avoiding contingencies caused by severe weather and half the usual breakage'. He boasted that they were the 'largest manufacturers of oven coke' and that orders to 'railways, maltsters, ironfounders and consumers' would be 'executed with probity, punctuality and dispatch'.

Child's activities, aided by Morden College and George Smith, made a visual impact on East Greenwich which continues, mainly because he built so much housing to a high standard.

The wharves, which he developed, are now built up with housing known as The River Gardens. His remit covered wharves known as Lovell's Wharf, Granite Wharf and Piper's Wharf along with Providence Wharf, Board of Works Wharf and Badcocks Wharf. Coles Child's original name for this riverside area was 'Greenwich Wharf'. In the succeeding years it was to house a wide range of riverside industries.

HOUSING

Having got the riverside industrial sites in place Coles Child turned to housing development. In the early 1840s he took over the rest of Great Meadow from Morden College with the condition that he drained ponds and dykes. Some portions of land were set aside for use in brick making. The first houses were built in 1842 and building continued for the next twenty years.

Sub-leases to builders were vetted by Morden College, before being awarded by Child. George Smith, as College Surveyor, monitored the design of the houses and in some cases made proposals himself.

There were sanctions against Child if substandard or unsuitable housing was built - for instance in 1853 he was told that no further leases would be granted unless some lower grade properties were abandoned. He was sometimes reprimanded for not sticking closely enough to Smith's designs.

THE DURHAM COALFIELD

The street names of the area reflect Coles Child's business interests. 'Pelton Road' is the main road through the estate and 'The Pelton Arms' on the corner was no doubt aimed at the thirsty crews of colliers and riverside workers. Pelton Main was a major colliery in the Durham coalfield - the source of the coal in which Coles Child dealt. Waldridge, the original name for Christchurch Way, was another colliery in the same area. Although some street names have changed most of the original names were taken from the Durham Coalfield

Banning Street was originally 'Chester (le Street) Street, a town in Durham near Pelton and Waldridge. Derwent Street is probably a reference to the River Derwent, which flows near Chester le Street, or to the Derwent Ironworks nearby. Thornley,

Whitworth and Caradoc are all names of coal mines elsewhere in the Durham coalfield. Braddyll, was the name of a coal owner after which a railway and, - today, - a preserved locomotive in the National Railway Museum are named.

Pelton Colliery from W.T.Hair, Views of the Collieries, 1844

At one time terraces within these roads had separate names and these too had coalfield related names. For example - 'Lambton Terrace' in Pelton Road referred to a colliery in the Durham coalfield, as did Stanley Terrace.

Although much of this housing is now in private hands, Morden College's distinctive plaque can still be seen on several buildings and is often mistaken for a fire insurance sign.

GREENWICH WHARF

Coles Child's coal business was concentrated on part of Greenwich Wharf – the area known as 'Lovells Wharf' until recently. Other wharves to the east were leased out to stone, barge building and river trades. He clearly did not intend to continue managing his wharfage business personally and he passed it into the hands of two managers, - William Whiteway and Frederick Rowton. It became known as Whiteway's Wharf. Both Whiteway and Rowton lived locally in Blackheath. In 1871 Whiteway moved into the newly built 11 Westcombe Park Road called Teign Villa. Frederick Rowton lived at 5 Westcombe Park Road, Meadowbank, which was next door but one to Whiteway. His house was later occupied by the Greenwich cement manufacturer, Hollick

Rowton came to an arrangement with 'Caradoc and Usworth' Colliery in order to meet competition from coal brought in by rail. These were two newly sunk pits in the north east of what is now Washington New Town in Co. Durham. Two sorts of coal from the pits were sold in Greenwich, 'Caradoc's Wallsend' and Jonasshon's Wallsend'. By the 1840s the use of the word 'Wallsend' was a generic term to describe good quality domestic coal.

Rowton and Whiteway also operated a cement works on the eastern part of Greenwich Wharf where there were lime kilns. Bricks were also made there.

Coles Child died at his home in Bromley in 1872 and the Greenwich Wharf business remained in the hands of Whiteway and Rowton. Whiteway left ten years later to become a Conservative Party activist in local politics. The cement business continued in operation on Greenwich Wharf. The eastern section of the wharf was passed to John Waddell

Waddell and Co are said to have built a 'dock' – presumably the inlet since known as 'Dead Dog Bay' . They too were coal merchants with an office at upmarket 14 Royal Parade in Blackheath. For a short time in the 1880s an ice merchant, John Ashby, rented part of the site and in the 1890s an ice well was built.

Coles Child's head lease on the whole site expired soon after the First World War and Morden College began a period of re-evaluation of the site. By 1918 the frontage was silting up rapidly. All around were houses and shops while inside the wharf were brick buildings including a stable for fourteen horses, with living rooms above. On the wharf was a travelling crane. The tenant was Yarmouth Carriers based in Hull. They left in the early 1920s, leaving behind them a 'Grafton crane'

SHAW LOVELL

Shaw Lovell leased most of the site in the late 1920s. They were a family business dating from 1869. Originally known as 'Bristol Steam Navigation Co. Ltd.' they employed as their General Traffic Agent, Charles Shaw Lovell. In 1908 the business was incorporated as 'C.Shaw Lovell & Sons Ltd. with City offices. They moved to Greenwich in 1911 becoming head lessees in the early 1920s.

Under Shaw Lovell the wharf was handling non-ferrous metals for transhipment into barges. In the 1920s the company dealt with scrap metal from First World War battlefields. The odd unexploded shell was, no doubt, only one of the hazards. There was also a sideline in the export of stone for war grave headstones. By the 1920s Shaw Lovell had their own ships: - Innisulva, Innishannan, Tower Bridge and Eiffel Tower. They also owned a tug and two lighters. On site there was a London Metal Exchange approved warehouse. In the 1960s Lovell House was built at the southern end of the wharf area as their head office. A large computer system was installed there. In 1975 these offices moved to Bristol and Lovell House was taken over by the Greater London Council for their educational social work service. It was demolished with the rest of the wharf around 2009. Nothing was saved, not even a commemorative plaque.

THE CRANES

In the 1970s a Butters' Crane from Custom House Quay, Dublin was brought to Greenwich and in the early 1980s a 20-ton Butters crane was installed, although as they were made in Glasgow, these structures really should he called 'Scotch Derricks'. Such equipment was once very common around the Port of London but has now almost completely disappeared

In 1982 the wharf handled 118,000 tons of cargo, steel, aluminium, galvanised sheeting and gas pipes as well as timber and some other items. In all this work the two cranes played a key role. They were a dramatic local feature - much photographed and the subject of many paintings and drawings. They proved difficult to research since the brass licence plates on them had vanished.

Shaw Lovell left the wharf and it remained empty, despite being 'safeguarded' for wharfage use. The cranes remained a popular feature and the Council agreed to tell potential developers to leave them on site as a feature. However, early one morning they were removed by Morden College, with no notice to the Council or anyone else.

The site was taken over by developers, London and Regional. The wharf was demolished and the current flats built. Local worries over the height of new blocks of flats led to a community campaign which managed to persuade developers to reduce the number of floors.

The name change to 'The River Gardens' from Greenwich Wharf – and indeed Lovell's – upset some. Developers, as ever, were required by the Council to use the River for removals and deliveries – and developers, as ever, bleated that they were unable to do it. It is cheering therefore to remember a community meeting where Mr.Enifer stood up to say that he had been foreman on the wharf, all his team were in the room – would the developers like some help in managing the wharfage?

THE COAL TRADE

This chapter has been about how 19th century development here was concentrated initially on the coal trade, and the history of one particular wharf involved in it.

In the 19th century coal ships from north east England, 'colliers', began to crowd the River, as more coal came from the North Eastern ports to supply London's industry.

Nearby Greenwich marsh were areas crucial to the organisation of the coal trade. In the 1830s, down river at Charlton, 'collier stands' were developed where ships waited their turn to go into wharves to unload. The system to regulate the incoming traffic, based on the Coal Exchange in London, was reordered in the early 1840s and one of the key buildings involved was The Harbour Master's house on Ballast Quay, adjacent to the site at which Coles Child was active.

No one should underestimate the importance of the coal trade to London, as without it the capital city would have remained medieval. Coal provided the power and raw materials that allowed the city to grow.

After 1870 the use of 'sea coal' from the Tyne ports escalated and it appealed to new customers who needed a regular large supply of coal. Large gas works and south east London because of this coal supply.

THE TELECOMMUNICATIONS REVOLUTION

Enderby Wharf is the next wharf as you travel downriver from the site developed by Coles Child for Morden College. Remarkably it still has the name of the Enderby family some 170 years after they left it. This had previously been the site of the Government gunpowder works and was almost the only site on the west bank riverside that did not, and does not, belong to Morden College. It also now, in 2019, the only site which still has a factory on it and one which is a recognisable descendant of the original factory here in the 1850s. The story of what happened here is remarkable

ROPE

Around 1800 a rope walk was built in Greenwich on the site of the old Government gunpowder depot. In the records a John Hounson is listed as the owner and he was probably the same man who had been the Clerk at the naval rope walk in Woolwich - and perhaps he had decide to set up his own business.

Rope is essential for a maritime nation. Rope factories are called 'rope walks' and they show up on old maps as long thin works. In the late 18th century rope makers worked by walking backwards with something like 40 lbs of fibre twisted round their waists which they twisted with their fingers to make the rope - and in every working day they walked more than 20 miles.

By 1808 Hounson had gone and a James Littlewood was there with a 'rope house, rope walk, houses and wharf'. Littlewood later described how he had borrowed £40 from friends in order to take the rope walk on but he was bankrupt by 1817. He had then handed the business over to "a person named Young" and was employed himself as foreman. Soon after he was sacked by Mr. Young for stealing hemp, and began a legal action to get the rope walk back. It emerged that at the time of this action he was actually a prisoner in Horsemonger Lane Jail in Southwark for operating an illicit liquor still and for selling the liquor in the prison. Mr.Young, who is otherwise unknown, kept the rope works and ran it for the next ten or so years.

The rope works was purchased in 1830 by the Enderby brothers, Charles, George and Henry. Over the next few years they developed the site by adding a sail making works and a hemp factory. The rope walk remained on site and can be seen marked on maps of the telegraph cable works into the 20th century. Its length could even still be made out from the Greenwich riverside path until 2014 or so but the layout of Barratt's high rise developments have now obliterated it.

'The Enderby Works and the Beale Foundry on an otherwise natural riverside

THE ENDERBY FAMILY

The Enderby family were very numerous but the brothers who bought the rope walk were descendants of the Samuel Enderby who had had an 'oil and white lead' works in Loman Street, in The Borough. He was in the 'oil and Russia' trade, which meant that he processed mutton fat from the Baltic, together with oil from whales slaughtered at sea, at a plant in Rotherhithe. Oil had all sorts of uses but, in the days before coal gas, was often used for street lighting.

Samuel married Mary Buxton whose family were ship owners and he took over her family business. His ships went out to hunt whales and by 1790 he was a rich man with sixty-eight whaling ships working in the Southern Oceans.

In the 1790s his son, Samuel, Jnr., lived in a large and impressive house on Crooms Hill. His mother lived on Blackheath and family members were active in local good causes. It was his sons who bought the Greenwich riverside site.

The factory consisted of two large waterside buildings where spinning machinery and looms were used to make canvas. On site were rooms to spin hemp and a flax mill. Outside was a building for a steam engine and boiler, houses for the foremen, stables, a smithy, and a joinery. There was a 'pitch house' and the brothers negotiated seven-year contracts with the gas companies for a supply of tar. There was also a project with the City of London Gas Company for making 'composition,' usually a coal tar based mortar used by the cheaper end of the building trade. In 1837 Michael Faraday himself gave a lecture in their works in 1837 on the use of naphtha as a solvent for rubber and how it could be applied to new types of rope and cable. Their most famous ship was the '*Samuel Enderby*'. For her first voyage an experimental rot proofing was used. This was Kyan's extremely poisonous sublimate solution, more usually used as a treatment for syphilis. Such uses of chemical products still under development in the 1830s show how open the Enderby brothers were to innovation and the new ideas about chemistry and its development.

This younger generation of Enderbys had money and leisure and many ideas, not only in the field of manufacture. Charles Enderby was one of the founders of the Royal Geographical Society. Enderby crews went to the Southern Oceans in search of whales and in the course of their travels made many important discoveries. Their ships became identified with Antarctic exploration and the stories of the explorers with their, sometimes harrowing, adventures make exciting reading. They named the new lands which they discovered 'Adelaide Island' after Queen Adelaide, 'Mount William', after William IV - and, of course, 'Enderby Land'.

Nevertheless the business was gradually failing.

The Enderby fire
Illustrated London News

On 8 March 1845, a devastating fire at Enderby Wharf put an end to the family's involvement in the sail and rope-making business. The factory's own fire engine fought the blaze joined by two from the Parish, another from the Royal Dockyard and one from the London Fire Brigade Establishment. A detachment of Royal Marines was sent to help but there was never very much hope of saving the ropewalk.

By the next morning all that remained were the 'lofty walls' of the factory - and they were blown down by the high winds in the next few days. It was said in the Kentish Mercury that the fire was either 'spontaneous combustion' or that it was 'wilfully raised by some incendiary'.

A small house which may have been on the riverside was also destroyed and by June 1845, building work began on a new riverside house for Charles Enderby, possibly on the foundations of the old house. The new house incorporated an unusual 'Octagon Room' on the first floor of the north-west corner with an angled bay window and river views. This building is Enderby House which still stands on the river bank. Charles entertained the rich and famous here. He had a number of 'curiosities' including a Tudor bedstead and a stuffed 'parson bird' from New Zealand, which, when alive, had been a pet.

Enderby House
When still in use by Alcatel pre 2010

The Enderbys were part of that circle of merchants with strong government and establishment links - the same people who ran Morden College and the East India Company. Exploration was an expensive business: in theory, it was undertaken to discover new areas for whale fishing but this trade was soon in decline as gas lighting replaced oil, and whales became scarcer.

In 1847 Charles Enderby got a concession to set up a whaling station in the Auckland Islands in Antarctica, the 'Southern Whale Fishery'. It was a short lived and unsuccessful venture in which he, and other members of his family, lost a lot of money and the brothers died in relative poverty.

TELEGRAPH CABLES AT MORDEN WHARF

The story starts a few hundred yards further north at Morden Wharf – now a development site. In the 1830s as Morden College began to parcel out sites to those who were willing to develop them this large area was let to a Charles Holcombe. He began to sub-let to 'suitable' industrial tenants. One of these was a William Kuper.

The story of the development and laying of submarine telegraph cables is complicated and involves many people and companies. The first cables were protected by twisted wires in a similar way to the 'wire rope', used for haulage in mines and quarries, and Johann Georg Wilhelm Küper was a manufacturer of this with works originally in Camberwell. In 1848 the company went into bankruptcy, and was acquired by its main customer, George Elliot.

Elliot had begun as a mining engineer working for the Durham coal owner, the Marquis of Londonderry. He had been advisor to Newall's of Gateshead where most of the early telegraph cables had been made. By 1851, Küper needed to expand and so leased the Morden Wharf site. That year, the first successful submarine telegraph cable which was to be laid across the English Channel was manufactured and a subcontract for the last 5 miles went to Küper to complete the project.

The success of this contract led Richard Atwood Glass, Elliot's accountant, to see an opportunity in protecting subsea cable with wire armouring. Many technical difficulties had to be overcome but some successes came and orders followed. At Greenwich Holcombe had erected a new building for them of a 'sound and substantial character' as Morden College had specified. Elliott then took Glass into partnership and W. Kuper and Co. became Glass, Elliot and Company.

An early commission was to make the cable for a submarine link between Northern Italy and Corsica and for this they made sheathing to cover a core which had already made by the Islington based Gutta Percha Company. For this a temporary jetty was built in 1854 to load cable onto SS Persian.

Glass Elliott works at Morden Wharf

The next cable was destined for a link across the Cabot Strait in America. Problems were encountered in loading the cable onto the ship from Morden Wharf and, to deal with this, cable pits were dug in which the cable was coiled up and tested underwater while it was still in storage. Contemporary drawings show the works at Morden Wharf with 'Glass Elliot, Submarine Cables' written on the roof of the main buildings, at an angle so as to be seen from the River. They also show two pits lined with bricks, and a bridge in-between with arched drainage ducts underneath. From these cables could be loaded on to the ship.

GLASS ELLIOTT AND THE MOVE TO ENDERBY WHARF

In 1857, Glass Elliot got a contract for armouring half of the cable for the first attempt to lay a cable across the Atlantic, and the Morden Wharf site was too small to accommodate the amount of cable which needed to be made. Glass Elliot made an agreement with another submarine cable manufacturer, William Thomas Henley to buy the derelict Enderby Hemp and Rope works. By 1859 Henley had left Greenwich and moved to North Woolwich. In 1864, Glass Elliot and Company merged with the Gutta Percha Company, to form The Telegraph Construction and Maintenance Co (known as Telcon) with John Pender as Chairman, Richard Glass as Managing Director and George Elliot and Daniel Gooch as board directors.

Gutta Percha is a natural product derived from trees grown in Malaya and elsewhere. It was discovered to be an effective insulator for underwater cables. Later Glass Elliott asked for permission to build a causeway at Enderby's together with another at the 'telegraph works' – still at Morden Wharf. So the long occupation of Enderby Wharf by Glass Elliott and their successors began. The works at Morden Wharf continued in use until the Morden College lease expired in 1895 and thenceforth manufacture was concentrated at Enderby Wharf. As part of the deal Morden College agreed to sell Telcon a small parcel of land, in the middle of the Telcon site. Known as Bendish Marsh it had been leased from the College since 1864.

While techniques for handling the cable were perfected, survey work went on for the laying of the Atlantic Telegraph cable. For this a new company, The Atlantic Telegraph Company, was set up in 1856. A telegraph link between the old and new worlds was seen as something of great importance – submarine cables were now being laid to link countries round the world, but a link to America was paramount. There was much excitement and it was recognised that it could change the way in which business and society were organised. Interest by the public was enormous on both sides of the Atlantic.

The core for the first Atlantic cable was made by the Gutta Percha Company and the job of making the sheathing was shared between Glass Elliott, in Greenwich, and Newall in Birkenhead. This sheathing used eighteen wires woven around a core separated by hemp and soaked in tar, pitch and linseed oil in a system said to have been designed by Brunel. Enough wire would be needed to encircle the earth three times. The cable was made in 1,200 pieces, each two miles long, which were then spliced together into eight lengths of 300 miles each. Work began on December 1856. Unfortunately it turned out that the cable made in Birkenhead had a right-handed twist, while Glass Elliott, gave theirs a left-handed twist. This, and other problems, took time to sort out.

It was necessary to design a new method of paying the cable out from the ships into the sea. This was to allow control over the speed of the cable as it left the ship, and so that it could be stowed efficiently. Half the cable was to be laid from Valentia, the westernmost point in Britain, on the Irish coast and the other half from Newfoundland. The Greenwich made cable went into the British naval ship, HMS Agamemnon. She was a 'wooden walled ship of the line' that and had been the flagship at the bombardment of Sevastopol. That the Government lent her to the Atlantic Telegraph for the project demonstrated quite clearly the level of their backing for this apparently private project. The cable was loaded from Greenwich in July 1857 and coiled into Agamemnon's hold by sailors sitting on stools, watching every inch of cable in case there were flaws in it.

Agamemnon and the cable had a magnificent send off with a garden-party in Erith for the crew and Glass Elliott's workmen but the attempt was a failure. The cable broke after only 300 nautical miles had been laid and was lost. The cable makers went back to Greenwich to start work again.

Glass Elliott was contracted to make a further 900 nautical miles of cable for the second attempt in the Atlantic. Once again the cable was loaded onto Agamemnon and, despite many difficulties;

it was successfully laid by August 1858, to rapturous acclaim in the press. Sadly the connection lasted just two months and by October nothing could be transmitted through it. Once again the cable makers returned to Greenwich and, it wasn't until 1864 that they were ready to try again. Telcon's technicians had designed a new and improved cable for the next attempt.

GREAT EASTERN

I.K. Brunel's Great Eastern off Sheerness - where she was loaded with cable

Following the second abortive attempt to achieve a working cable across the Atlantic Telcon set about making a new Atlantic cable which would be more robustly constructed, heavier, and nearly double the diameter. There would be seven strands of high purity copper, six of them twisted round the seventh and there would be four layers of gutta percha. Between the copper and the gutta percha there would be a layer of resin and tar. As it was made, inch by inch, it was closely inspected because a break would mean another expensive disaster. The new cable was so big and heavy that Agamemnon could not carry it and it was thought three ships would be needed.

The solution was the SS Great Eastern. Launched seven years before from Millwall and, known as 'The Leviathan', she was designed to be bigger and more powerful than any ship before her. She had failed as a passenger liner and was thus bought very cheaply by Brunel's friend, Daniel Gooch, while he was a director of Great Western Railway Company. He promptly joined the Board of the Telegraph Construction Company and offered Great Eastern to them for shares in the Atlantic Telegraph Co

There was even greater interest in this new, third, cable and the Prince of Wales visited Greenwich to see it being manufactured. He sent a message through the 1,400 miles then being tested in the factory - 'I wish success to the Atlantic Cable'.

The Prince of Wales' visit

It took eight months to make the new cable and two weeks to load it into *Great Eastern*. The ship was so big that she could not be brought alongside Morden or Enderby Wharves and every bit of cable had to be ferried out to her and loaded off Sheerness. She left Greenwich for Valentia on 15th July 1865 carrying 21,000 tons dead-weight.

When they were 948 miles from Valentia and 717 miles from their destination, Heart's Content in Newfoundland, the cable was once more broken and lost overboard. Four times the cable was found on the ocean bottom, and four times it slipped away. Then storms set in and the cable was thought to be lost. For a while, in England, it was also believed that the Great Eastern herself had gone down and once the cable was lost no messages could be got back. Once again, the cable makers went back to Greenwich.

TRY AGAIN

The Atlantic Telegraph Co was unable to raise new capital so Gooch and Pender raised £650K to launch the Anglo-American Telegraph Co. Each invested £10K and became directors, with Richard Atwood Glass becoming chairman of this new company.

The Telegraph Construction and Maintenance Co. made yet another new cable, which was finished in 1866. Once again they loaded the Great Eastern and once again she left the Thames for Valentia.

The bands on shore played 'Goodbye Sweetheart' as she left with 2,730 miles of cable. This time, on 27th July, she reached Heart's Content and the cable was laid at last to great celebrations.

Great Eastern then went back to look for the broken cable lost in the previous attempt. There was no way to contact the ship once she had left but on 2nd September the instruments at the Valentia end of the broken cable began to move. Staff on board Great Eastern had found the broken end two miles down, fished it up, and it too was now connected.

Within a few moments, both Europe and America knew where Great Eastern was and what she had done. It is one of the defining moments of the modern world.

The cable arrives at Heart's Content

It is difficult to overstate the importance of the Atlantic cable and the 'profound transformation' to which it led. It has been said that 'despite the romance of the workshop of the world ... it is in the under-publicised accounts department that the long-term future held sway'. The telegraph was a major agent of change and an instrument whose importance was not lost on City business interests, which controlled land on the Greenwich Peninsula and the companies, which made and laid the cable. The Stock Exchange was transformed by it, and by 1871 'trading on exchanges in New York and London were effectively integrated'. Within another two years connections were made to Tokyo and Melbourne and world markets were shifting towards globalisation.

At the end of the 20th century there was much talk about the global communications revolution. The real revolution came a hundred and sixty eight years ago when wires twisted on Greenwich marsh crackled into life on the sea bed. It is said that for many years one of the Great Eastern's masts stood on Enderby Wharf as a reminder of what had been achieved.

Of all the sites involved with the cables only one has an exhibition to show what happened - at Heart's Content in Newfoundland although there has been talk of a World Heritage site between there and Valentia.

TELCON AND ITS SUCCESSORS

The submarine cable works at Enderby Wharf was to prosper greatly and by the 1920s they had made the vast majority of underwater telegraph cables around the world - no other works came near them in output. There have been several changes of company names and management but the works continues, for some years in French ownership and is now owned by Nokia. The research facilities at Greenwich have kept it in the forefront and many new technologies have emerged, in particular optical fibre transmission for which Charles Kao received a Nobel Prize in 2009. There was also development of specialist materials – for example, Mu Metal and Telcothene, a polythene.

In over 150 years work this site has been of vast importance internationally and has provided the revolutionary technology which today we take for granted. In the 1860s, cables transmitted a few messages in Morse at 18-12 words a minute; today fibre optic cables carry terabits of data that support the vast traffic on the Internet.

For many years the cable laying ships and repair ship were moored alongside river structures called dolphins. Some of the loading gear, installed in the 1950s still remains on the jetty as a monument to 162 years of the manufacture of submarine cable systems on Greenwich Marsh. The wharf is no longer used, and the 'dolphins' for the cable shipsthat were loaded here are gone. The John W. Mackay, a cable ship preserved there for many years, was towed away 1989 to the breakers yard.

AND NOW

In the early 21st century Alcatel, by then owners of the works, sold the River frontage to a developer for housing. The developer then went bankrupt and the area was left with no security. The original developer had planned a major terminal for cruise liners on the riverside but no work on this was ever done. A major public campaign began against the berthing of ships here, because of their use of polluting diesel power while moored there. This appears to have been resolved when the current owners admitted there were no plans for the terminal.

Enderby House itself had been used as offices by the cable companies and was not in bad condition if a bit 'tired'. Once in the ownership of the developer it was neglected and was squatted, burnt, and left to rot.

As a result a campaign group was formed, the Enderby Group, to try and save the house and get it used so as to reflect some of the telecoms heritage of the area. A new housing developer, Barratt's, took over and soon the riverside area was covered in large blocks of flats. People began to move in.

Enderby House – derelict.

Enderby Group seminar about the history of the wharf

The planning consent for the flats required Enderby House to be restored and Barratts stabilised the property and restored the exterior. It was then announced that it would become a pub operated by Young's brewery. We wait to see what will happen but the hoped for telecoms heritage centre seems near impossible to achieve.

Alongside Enderby House was an office building with decorative cable and gutta percha motifs above the lintels and door. This was demolished and no features kept. Also demolished was a chimney which may have originated in the works used by Joshua Taylor Beale. On the riverside are the cable-loading remains on the jetty and some steps into the River, covering a medieval sluice, and on them is a carving depicting the history of cable manufacture and it is hope that this will remain. Barrett's commissioned a sculpture which will stand outside Enderby House. Lay Lines, by Bobby Lloyd, is designed to display cross sections of cable as tables and chairs. There is also an electronic information system.

THIS IS ALL ABOUT COAL TAR

To return to the mid-19th century: George Smith and the Mercers Company's holdings on the Marsh. His energy and initiative transformed Greenwich Marsh, and much else in Greenwich beside. Site after site was parcelled up, a developer found, and the site leased with clear instructions for good quality buildings and respectable sub-tenants.

It is also remarkable that most of these chosen leaseholders were making an investment themselves in industries dependent on coal tar – a waste product of the new gas industry. Gas industry waste products in the period are usually thought of as a nuisance, polluting, dangerous and an expensive problem. However coal tar was being bought, processed and used as a raw material by people who had every expectation of making a lot of money.

There were many experiments and ideas about what the tar could be used for. Use on weatherproofing ships was one obvious idea, as was replacing imported 'Stockholm' wood based tar for items like rope. Many experimented with paints and varnishes, as well as pavements and paths – with some giving an impression that their raw material was Swiss bitumen. One experimenter had an application for coffins. Most successful and most common however were those who used it as a wood preservative, and succeeded in impregnating the wood with it,

These industrialists needed the processing ability of the gas industry. It might be said that the Greenwich Peninsula was made by what it is now on the one hand by George Smith and Morden College and on the other hand by the early gas industry. This does not involve the gas works which later came to the Peninsula with their massive tar works at Ordnance Wharf. That was much later and in a whole different world. The tar came from the many small gas works that sprung up in London and the surrounding area after 1815.

BRYAN AND HOWDEN

John Bryan and Gidley Howden were almost the earliest potential industrials tenants identified by Morden College. They had a works on Bankside and wanted to expand. They made coal gas manufacturing apparatus, being one of many companies in the iron trade who were then taking advantage of the rapidly expanding gas industry. A third partner in the business, who probably provided the finance, was a Charles Holcombe.

John Bryan had been responsible for the building and setting up of a number of gas works throughout southern England, with varying degrees of financial success and subsequent recriminations from local people. One was set up in Maldon in 1839. In this he was typical of several operators in this trade. Gidley Howden had been involved in developing a 'patent stove' and appears to have been an enthusiastic Methodist.

In 1837 Bryan and Howden took a ninety nine year lease on a plot, previously used to grow osier, to the north of Great Pitts – part of the area which is today Morden Wharf. Anything they built needed to be approved by George Smith. Problems soon began to arise.

In 1839 Morden College discovered that they were unable to obtain insurance on the site because of the 'extremely hazardous business' being carried out there. This was tar distilling and it was reported that the premises 'consists of three brick buildings - one a cooperage, another for the boiler and rectifying plant, and another for the tar still'. By this time coal tar from the gas industry was available at knock-down prices and the flourishing shipbuilding industries were markets for the products. Throughout the area many entrepreneurs were experimenting with cheap coal tar in the hope of making a saleable product.

Tar in use - tar dipping at Glass Elliott

Complaints began to be made about the nature of Bryan and Howden's work from several quarters and it appeared that 'oily matter was running about'. The partnership was in financial trouble and Charles Holcombe wrote to Morden College to say that he no longer had any connection with the partnership which was dissolved in 1839.

In 1841 Morden College offered the site to other potential tenants. One offer came from Holcombe himself and another from an Arthur Hills of Battersea. He was the brother of Frank Hills and, as we shall see, the Hills family was to make their fortunes from gas industry waste products – as Bryan and Howden had tried to do and failed. The first tenant had been a failure; others were to do rather better.

CHARLES HOLCOMBE

In 1841 Morden College granted a lease on a large site - 'Further Pitts' - to Charles Holcombe who had taken over some of the land previously leased to Bryan and Howden and was adding to it more land in the northern part of the Morden Wharf site. Like Coles Child, Holcombe acted as a developer, leasing part of the site to a network of other companies.

Holcombe was a rich man - only three years earlier he had taken occupation of Valentines Park, a large mansion in Ilford. He had previously been the tenant of Hatcham Manor Farm at New Cross, owned by the Haberdashers' Company and on the site of the fire station in Queens Road. There was mention of a catgut factory 'in the summer house.... offensive and disgusting'. Holcombe actually lived somewhere rather grander - Porchester Terrace. He was one of the family who had owned the Blackhorse Brewery from at least the 16th century at Maze Pond in the Borough on the site of what is now Guy's Hospital cancer centre. Charles Holcombe inherited it and sold it in the same year in which he bought Valentines. A road alongside Valentine's House is named after him 'Holcombe Road'. Strangely, the adjacent road is 'Bethell Avenue' – John Bethell's work on the Peninsula is described below.

In Greenwich directories Holcombe's works on the marsh is given as a 'brass foundry, tar and Asfelt works. He is also described as a 'refiner of coal tar, spirit, pitch and varnish'. So, like many others in the 1840s, he was experimenting with gas industry tars for use in paint and varnish.

Holcombe built Morden Wharf. It is not known why he called it this - perhaps he had a special relationship with Morden College, or wanted to curry favour with them. He built a road, known as Morden Lane or Morden Wharf Road which still runs through the area although it no longer gives access to the River. Around 1848, he had a public house built close to the riverfront. This was the 'Sea Witch' accessed by a short lane, which became known as Sea Witch Lane.

Like Coles Child, Holcombe wanted to improve the property which he had leased and gave this as his reason when he asked Morden College for permission to lay asphalt on the river path. He also asked permission to build a draw dock and complained when permission had been given to someone else to deposit rubbish on the riverside. He built houses, inevitably designed by George Smith of Morden College.

These activities gradually added to the local amenities and made the area more attractive to other incoming industrialists.

WILLIS AND WRIGHT

Another partnership which acted as a developer was Willis and Wright, the owners of Champion's Vinegar Brewery on the corner of Old Street and City Road in Shoreditch. Elizabeth Champion was a signatory to the lease. In the 1840s they were had the area of Greenwich Marsh known as 'Horseshoe Breach'- later known as Bay Wharf and the site of the working boatyard.

By 1845 Willis and Wright had built 'a tar factory, house, chemical factory, and buildings' followed by complaints about leakage of 'noxious matter' from the plant. It is not clear why vinegar makers should open a tar distillery but in 1846 they advertised 'vinegar, mustard, acetic acid and naphtha'. Naphtha is oil distilled from coal tar – which is a very different substance to mustard and vinegar. Willis and Wright signed a lease with Morden College in 1850 with the usual expectation on by College's that they would undertake development work at Horseshoe Breach. The site was inspected by George Smith and discussions on the work began. A year went by and nothing happened while complaints continued. Ten years later Morden College said that nothing had been done.

Willis and Wright left Greenwich in the early 1860s having let some sub tenancies. Horseshoe Breach had an interesting future in other hands.

JOHN BETHELL

It is not clear exactly when John Bethell first moved to his site on the west bank of the Marsh. The earliest correspondence in the Morden College archive dates from 1839 when he made an offer for 20 acres of land and was turned down. Two months later he was negotiating with them on buildings to be erected and the route of a road. His tenancy with them must be almost the longest on the Marsh, since his successor company, The Improved Wood Paving Co., lasted well into the 20th century – and is still shown on maps in the 1930s.

Bethell pioneered one of the most successful processes for tar use in the 1830s. He was a barrister from Bristol and the brother of Lord Chancellor, Richard Bethell. He was to exploit his process on a Morden College owned site on the west bank of Greenwich Peninsula.

In 1848 Bethell patented a way of *'preserving animal and vegetable substances from decay'*. There was a great need to find a way of preserving wood from rot and the Earl of Dundonald had suggested the usefulness of coal tar for this in the 1780s. Other inventors had used other preservatives and other methods; Bethell was to take some elements of each to achieve his object.

One particular need was for a cheap way of preserving wooden ships. The eventual success of Bethell's process was to lead to the worldwide use of wood for such things as railway sleepers and telegraph poles. At Greenwich the works eventually specialised in the manufacture of tar soaked wood block paving. The process which Bethell developed involved an apparatus first designed in Paris. The dried timber was put on iron bogey frames, run into a strong iron cylinder, and the air pumped out. The preservative solution was then forced in. Although a number of preservatives were specified coal tar was the cheapest and easiest to obtain. It was also far safer to use than some of the other recommended substances, as for instance Kyan's sublimate which was poisonous and particularly dangerous. Bethell seems to have either sold his patent to others or licensed them to use it.

Bethell had originally set up in business with a tar distillery in Battersea in 1845 but this was burnt down two years later. He expanded with a chemical works at Bow Common, and another near Blackwall Point on a site leased from Morden College. His first approach to Morden College had been as early as 1839 when he asked for the use of a piece of rough ground. He gave his address as Mecklenberg Square in Bloomsbury, built by the Greenwich Hospital Estates surveyor, Joseph Kaye. His Greenwich works was soon underway and coal tar was purchased in bulk from the Imperial Gas Company works at St. Pancras and Haggerston.

There were soon a number of works in East London area which preserved wood using Bethell's methods. The most successful and best known were Burt, Boulton and Haywood whose enormous tar processing plant was based in Silvertown on the Essex bank of the Thames.

The Greenwich works remained in operation for many years. After Bethell's death in the 1870s his wife Louisa retained ownership, although she lived in Bath while professional managers ran the company from an address in King William Street, City of London. In the 1880s the works was transferred to the Improved Wood Pavement Company in which the Bethell family remained involved.

Bethel's process was successful and long lasting and one from which many other manufacturers did very well. Wooden road blocks were just one of a number of important applications – telegraph poles, railway sleepers, and much else depended on the preservative qualities of the tar and the ability to impregnate the wood with it.

Many other manufacturers on the Peninsula used gas industry by-products, as part of their processes – if not so directly as in wood preservation.

FRANK HILLS

Frank Clark Hills made a fortune out of the gas industry. Tar does not seem to be one of his main interests; nevertheless he showed where money could be made out of gas industry waste. Several of his activities were also undertaken by others in the area – and he is thus a good introduction to a wider industrial world. In any case busy, inventive, secretive, unscrupulous Frank is someone that should not be missed.

When Frank died in 1892 his death initially went more or less unnoticed – with only short obituaries 'Death of local chemical manufacturer' in the local papers. It was not until 29th July of that year that The Times carried a report of his will and it turned out this south London chemical manufacturer had left a personal fortune of £1,942,836 11s. 11d., a phenomenal sum in the 1890s.

The tide mill on the east bank has already come to our attention. In the early 1840s the entire estate – mill, cottages, house, pub and land were all bought by Frank Hills.

It is also of note that Frank was just the most dominant member of a large family of brothers – of which he roughly in the middle – the third son. Most of them appear to have been in the same trade as chemical manufacturers and business men. They were spread all over the country with important works in, for instance, Anglesey and Newcastle. They had mines in Spain, and eventually controlled most of the British salt industry. Their sons and sons-in-law took on more enterprises all interconnected. Frank's own third son, Arnold, became Chair of a leading world-class ship building company and founded West Ham Football Club.

Frank and his brothers were the sons of Thomas Hills who had had a chemical works in Bromley by Bow and who had possibly pioneered a number of processes. This included one for the manufacture of sulphuric acid although this was open to some challenge as to its origins. Frank had taken over a chemical works on Deptford Creek, hitherto owned by a German called Beneke who had developed there an important process for the manufacture of sulphuric acid. Frank was afterwards usually described as 'the Deptford chemist' although his works on the Peninsula was much larger.

The family had at least one previous attempt to take over premises on the Peninsula. In 1840 'A Hills of Battersea Fields' – Frank's brother Arthur - had applied to lease an existing chemical works from Morden College and an Edwin Hills, also of Battersea Fields, applied again in 1845.

The tide mill was set to be sold by auction in June 1842 and this may be when it was acquired by Frank Hills. However it is said to have purchased as part of his marriage settlement, although his marriage to Ellen Rawlings was not until 1847 and there may have been an earlier mortgage.

One non-chemical and non-gasworks related activity of Frank around this time was the manufacture of road vehicles – cars propelled by steam power. He had developed two of these but it is far from clear where these vehicles were manufactured except that it was said to be in Greenwich.

In 1833 a Mr. Roberts of Manchester had built a steam road vehicle which included a compensating gear which he patented in 1832. Frank Hills patented some developments of the idea in 1843 and it has been widely suggested that he infringed Roberts' rights. It was also noted that in 1839 Frank Hills had travelled on one of Walter Hancock's coaches, 'Automaton' on its inaugural run and 'was doubtless taking a lesson in steam carriage construction during the journey'.

Frank Hills' steam carriage.
(Drawing thanks to the late Patrick Hills)

Joshua Taylor Beale was making similar vehicles around the same time for Francis Macaroni and it may be that Frank's cars were made by him too. He is not known to have had any engineering capacity in his works based on the old tide mill.

From 1845 the mill was described as 'a steam flour mill' and perhaps the tide mill itself was replaced by a steam engine. In 1895 the mill contained a "pair of vertical inverted oscillating steam engines by Joyce of Greenwich". William Joyce's factory was alongside Deptford Creek near where Waitrose is today. He had died in 1856 so these engines must have been about forty years old and may in fact have been the engines already installed when Frank took over the mill.

On the riverbank to the north of the mill Frank erected a chemical works. This was gradually extended, as for instance in 1869 when an ammonia plant was built. What sort of chemicals were made at East Greenwich? Almost certainly sulphuric acid was made here. One very good source of information about this works are the reports of inspectors and enquiries which took place as public complaints multiplied. A smell of 'an acid and sickening character' was complained of. This could be discerned not only in Greenwich and Charlton but 'appeared to annoy the garrison at Woolwich', three or four miles away!

We will later come to more works on the Peninsula which this inspector found to be a bit smelly. In doing so we will encounter more manure – and some guano – works.

At Frank's East Greenwich works there was also a manure manufactory and for this there were two 30 foot long steam boilers with a chimney as well as an 'Archimedean screw' and a bone crusher. The manure was made from 'shoddy', waste leather, dry bones, bone ash and refuse from sugar bakers - that is whatever organic rubbish could be bought cheaply. It was then piled up and mixed with sulphuric acid.

This process had been developed at a works on Deptford Creek by F.C. Lawes at a site slightly down stream of the Beneke Works taken over by Frank Hills. There are however some indications that Frank may have worked with or for Lawes and may have taken over some of the business.

The smell can be imagined (perhaps better if it is not!). In 1871 Mr. Pink, the Medical Officer of Health for Greenwich, began to give 'advice' designed for 'abatement of the nuisance which these works could scarcely have failed to occasion'. The agricultural journals of the time carry many many advertisements for Hills' manure. – For instance – "Superphosphate of Lime, Wheat, Corn, Grass, and Hop Manures, &c., are manufactured by F. C. Hills at the Chemical and Artificial Manure Works, Deptford and East Greenwich. These Manures will be found equal or superior to any other'

It seems a wide variety of chemicals were made at East Greenwich but that there was a concentration on things made from gas works wastes. At the 1851 Great Exhibition at Crystal Palace in Hyde Park Frank Hills won prizes for his ammonia salts and 'gas tar'. The tar, of course, came from one of the nearby gas works and was processed into a variety of oils, as well as pitch and asphalt. Hills' works specialised in ammonia salts which were made from gasworks' 'ammoniacal liquor'. He bought large amounts of this from almost every gasworks in London.

Frank Hills held many patents and one with which he made a great deal of money was for the 'purification' of newly-made coal gas to make it fit to be burnt for lighting in people's homes. He had patented this process against fierce competition from other industrial chemists and was to defend it vigorously in interminable court cases as he and the others sued each other, and then sued again, for infringement of their rights.

His method was to sell a gas company a licence to use the process which he had patented but had not developed himself. He would then sell them the mixture required to purify the gas and then ask for more money to remove it. He could then use the residue to manufacture chemicals for sale. Understandably this was disliked by the gas industry in general while making him extremely rich

This process left a valuable waste product from which sulphuric acid could be made, and in 1865, special tanks were installed at East Greenwich for storing this. Other acids were made on site-

nitric, tartaric and oxalic - as well as dyes. The same processes were used in the various works owned by his brothers and nephews around the country together with other works. This included salt works, a number of specialist chemical plants and some mines in Wales and elsewhere,

Chemicals were shipped out, and raw materials came in. Boats came from Spain delivering materials from Hills' mines, as well as materials from his brothers' factories in Newcastle and Anglesey, North Wales and elsewhere. It was all very profitable.

When Frank died in the 1890s his death was soon followed by those of his two elder sons – leaving his third son, vegetarian activist Arnold as his principle heir. Arnold is best known for founding West Ham Football Club in his role as Chair of Thames Ironworks.

There is much much more to be said about Frank, his work and his legacies. He himself chaired Thames Ironworks – probably the premier builder of warships world wide – for thirty years. His railway in Huelva in Spain is now a tourist attraction. In researching him I have always known there is much more to be discovered about this clever, ruthless, secretive man.

To return to Greenwich Peninsula – Frank's Chemical Works was sold to South Metropolitan Gas and was operated as their Phoenix Chemical Works – becoming one of the last areas of the East Greenwich Gas Works to be closed.

ENGINEERS

GUNS AND STEEL

Some of the most prominent Greenwich firms were in the engineering business and away from the Peninsula were some world class companies - like John Penn's marine engine factory on Blackheath Hill - who were developers of major pieces of equipment. Two preserved steam engines which were made on Greenwich Marsh remain today.

JOSHUA TAYLOR BEALE

Joshua Taylor Beale was versatile and ingenious, a classic engineer of the period. He had begun in Wapping where he took out a patent for 'improvements' to the design of a rotary steam engine. He moved to Greenwich in the 1830s and leased a site from the Enderby brothers at the western end of their works, the area where the boiler house and chimney stood until 2010.

Beale appears initially to have been designing and selling oil lamps. Like others he was buying gasworks' waste tar describing it as 'substances not usually burnt in such vessels'. He developed a means of heating inflammable liquids without any risk of them catching fire - important for those who wanted to work with coal tar. In 1834 he patented lamps which burnt 'the commonest hydrocarbon obtained from coal tar' and in 1837 came the 'Air and Vapour Light; where the oil was vapourised to mix with 'oxygen from the atmosphere'.

Beale lived in Conduit House on Trafalgar Road at the bottom of Vanburgh Hill – now the site of the old Granada Cinema converted into flats. There he brought up a family, a son and two daughters.

In 1835 he again patented his 'rotative engine' and installed it in a boat. A trial of it at Yarmouth was described by no less than George Stephenson who said the engine could not be made to work and the party was stranded out at sea. Beale, however, claimed to have sold 'a considerable number' of engines.

He patented a propeller for boats and a means of preventing 'encrusting' in boilers using urine and soda. He tried to make gas cookers - at a time when such things were quite unheard of and, allegedly, sent spies to see the kitchen equipment which a rival, Thomas Barlow, had installed in Islington

In, 1840 Beale, like Frank Hills, elsewhere on the Peninsula, was developing steam road vehicles. In the early 1840s at least two cars were made at Beale's Greenwich works. He was commissioned to do this by Col. Francis Maceroni who had had experience with steam road vehicles since the late 1820s and had manufactured them in Paddington. In 1841 Maceroni set up the 'Common Road Steam Conveyance Company' and asked Beale to build a vehicle , which he did with the help of his brother, Benjamin. A correspondent to Mechanics Magazine described a Greenwich factory where two 'handsome and powerful' carriages were being built.

Hills, Beale and Maceroni began to make demonstration trips around the Kentish countryside. In July 1840 a party of seventeen went in Maceroni's carriage from East Greenwich through Lewisham to Bromley. Returning they went up Blackheath Hill - at 12 miles per hour 'in gallant style'. They continued up Shooters Hill and as they needed 'water' they stopped at The Bull where 'the men were regaled and eulogised the scientific engineer'. Frank Hills' carriage went further - Windsor, Brighton, Hastings - although they had to stop every eight miles to take on water. Beale was to be paid £800 each for the carriages and because of the changes necessary to the design; he charged an extra £300 each. The money was not paid, Beale impounded the carriages and no more was heard of them

Beale's Exhauster

Most importantly Beale patented a piece of equipment called an 'exhauster'. Exhausters could be used in the gas works to draw the gas through the pipes like a pump and was an adaption of his rotary steam engine. One local customer was the South Metropolitan Gas Company in the Old Kent Road which bought an exhauster from Beale in 1854.

Joshua died in 1866 and the factory was taken over by his son, John. John Beale redesigned the exhauster and took out a new patent for it in the 1860s. However, the lease on the Greenwich factory was about to expire and John did not renew it. He went on to develop a number of inventions, a bicycle, and a sort of projector – but they were made elsewhere and by others.

The exhauster was extremely useful and profitable. John had sold the patent to the Bermondsey based Brian Donkin and it became a major part of his company's output. In 1903 Donkin left London for Chesterfield where they continued to pioneer new developments in gas industry machinery. Machinery based on Beale's exhauster patent was still being made in the 1960s'.

However once it became clear how valuable the patent was, Joshua's brother Benjamin emerged to challenge John's inheritance of it. He was aware that Joshua had never actually married John's mother and suggested John could not therefore have been left either the factory or the patents. Following a long legal action, he sold the original patents to Gwynne's engineers of Holborn and Hammersmith

Beale also designed and built a more conventional condensing beam engine. One of these was made in his Greenwich foundry, and installed in the Glemsford Silk Mill in Suffolk. It is now preserved in the Beamish Industrial Museum collection in County Durham.

APPLEBY BROTHERS

Another engineering firm with works on the peninsula could not have been more different from Beale.

Appleby Brothers were perhaps the largest general engineering company to come to East Greenwich. They were already a successful company and presumably wanted to expand to a larger site in the London area. They leased a site from Morden College in 1879 and also took over some of the site later known as Victoria Wharf, now Hansons, which had previously been used by Bessemer. They stayed there until 1910 and were to call it Star Wharf.

Appleby had been set up in 1782 at the Renishaw Iron works in Derbyshire. One of the founder's sons, Charles, opened his own engineering works at Emerson Street in Southwark, and in 1886, moved it to Greenwich. At the same time they maintained a works in Leicester.

Appleby's catalogue shows a wide range of goods, which they claimed to manufacture at Greenwich and/or Leicester. They made railway locomotives and supplied the 2'8" gauge 'Edith' to Robert Campbell of Farringdon in 1871 and 'Jessie' to the Manor Lime and Cement Works, Halling. They also made steam engines and in the 1880s they supplied engines to two single screw ships built in Holland for Watkins Tugs, Australia and Zealandia.

Cranes and hoists may have been their most important product and they exhibited them in Paris in 1876 and Vienna in 1873.

The firm was wound up in 1895 but the works came under the control of the Crayford based armaments company, Vickers, Son and Maxim. They acquired the Temperly Transporter Co, in 1908 and a transporter was installed at the adjacent Ordnance Wharf Tar Works. The focus of their activity began to move away from Greenwich and in 1910 the Greenwich works was at last closed.

The Appleby Works in Greenwich

Two Appleby engines have survived, one of which is now preserved locally at Crossness Engines Museum. The other is at the Forncett St.Mary Steam Museum in Norfolk. Many Appleby engines are preserved abroad, particularly in Australia and New Zealand. Four Appleby beam engines made in 1883 were used for pumping water in Albury, Bathurst, Goulburn and Wagga Wagga in New South Wales. A complete and working beam engine is kept at the Goulburn Historic Waterworks Museum in its original pump house with the two boilers originally used to power it.

AND IN THE BACK STREETS

There were, as everywhere, back street businesses in East Greenwich and the Marsh. Many of them were effectively small repair workshops servicing local vehicles and business needs. Many had begun as small forges. Most of them called themselves 'engineers'.

One of the longest lasting of these small scale East Greenwich industries was at the back of the riverside wharves in Derwent Street. James Ashbridge had a forge and smith's shop there before 1870 and a hundred years later his successors, by now 'motor body builders', were still on site. This is a consistent pattern - the small forge which is now a small motor repair shop. A site in Derwent Street is marked as 'Thames Foundry' on 19th century maps, and it is possible that Ashbridge was there as a successor to the original occupant, Percival Parsons, whose career will be outlined later. The site is now a row of houses.

Some small industries seem to have operated from people's homes - an example was Walter Cooper, listed as a patentee of Steam Traps. Did he manufacture the traps in his Pelton Road home or was this just an advertisement for his office and his business was elsewhere?

Another small works was Flavell, Butler, Montgomery, and Churchill, an engineering firm based in Bellot Street. Their type of work can be seen from a 1914 quotation to the London County Council for the construction of a working platform for a sludge loading plant on the Southern Outfall Sewer. In the 1920s they repaired a 'Grafton crane' which had been left behind by previous occupants at Lovells Wharf. Their site is now housing, called Flavell's Mews.

BESSEMER

In the 1860s industries on the Greenwich Peninsula took off with astonishing speed. Suddenly big names started to arrive. First it was shipbuilders, but then steel works and big guns moved in. With these industries, as with some others of the same era, backers came from the world of international banking.

This was a time when some major companies moved to the west bank of the Peninsula. Some of them seem to have been unduly secretive and it is also clear that there was a measure of liaison between at least two of them.

Henry Bessemer's method of steel production - his 'converter' - is usually associated with the north of England, and Sheffield in particular. But Bessemer lived in South London and built a steel works at Greenwich. Information about this works has proved elusive and there is some conflict of evidence about what really went on there. So, we need to ask what was Bessemer really doing at East Greenwich?

Henry Bessemer came from a French background and was an ingenious inventor who held numerous patents on all sorts of devices and processes from which he made a lot of money. One of the earliest was 'bronze powder', which he made in a factory near St. Pancras. He described some of the lengths he went to in order to keep the process secret and, in much the same vein, his unfinished autobiography is often very difficult to disentangle. Historians have suggested that his steel making process arose from his interest in making guns, something that, of course, would draw him to Woolwich and the Arsenal.

Bessemer had been in France working with the French military authorities when he came to the conclusion that a new sort of metal was needed. In due course he developed his process. To cut a very long story very short indeed - he became involved with Col. Eardley Willmot at the Royal Arsenal and plans were made to build a plant there for the manufacture of Bessemer's steel.

It soon became clear that this support was not shared by the Minister of War and Bessemer's steel was rejected for use in the Arsenal. Bessemer was very bitter 'it was quite clear that neither I, nor my steel, was wanted at Woolwich, and I made up my mind to leave the place severely alone in future'. The position at Woolwich was further complicated by the appointment in 1859 of William Armstrong; the Newcastle based arms manufacturer, to the position of Director of Rifled Ordnance at Woolwich.

Bessemer's son added a final, posthumous, chapter to Bessemer's autobiography. This chapter contains the only mention of the steel works that Bessemer had built at Greenwich in the late 1860s. The works was on the site more recently known as Victoria Wharf, today in use by Hanson's.

The new works took two years to lay out, and Percival Parsons, later to develop 'manganese bronze' was appointed Engineer and supervised the work. A jetty was built following an application from 'Bessemer Brothers' for permission from the Thames Conservators. An advertisement in the *Kentish Mercury* mentioned the closeness of the Bessemer works and its thirsty steelworkers to the Star in the East pub.

The works was very small and it was apparently intended to be run by Bessemer's sons. Its manager was Richard Price Williams, a railway engineer who was involved in using steel for rails. Bessemer Jnr says, "It had two 2½ ton converters and all the plant necessary. Including one 2½-ton steam hammer and another ... the buildings were carefully designed, with the intention that the establishment should be in all respects be a model one". He went on to explain that it was, never opened because of the "down turn in Thames shipbuilding"

The eventual fate of the Greenwich steel works is not clear. Bessemer Jnr. said that both works and plant were let to the London Steel and Ordnance Co.

'Henry Bessemer' continues to be listed in official records. In 1872 there was a complaint from Morden College that the 'Bessemer Steel Co.' had encroached on their land. Mysteriously, in 1874, 'Bessemer's liquidators' appear in the rate books. At the same time discussions had begun for Bessemer to lease 'a small field in the marshes' from Morden College for 21 years and they were delighted to learn that he was offering more than the market value for it, hardly the action of someone who does not want a site. As late as 1891 Morden College's surveyor was still dealing with 'Bessemer Brothers'.

From about 1878 all, or part, of the works was let to Appleby Brothers and almost twenty years later, the site was let to a linoleum manufacturer who later bought the freehold. The really interesting thing is what the linoleum manufacturer had to say about the site.

His name was Frederick Walton and perhaps he knew Henry Bessemer – another of Bessemer's interests was linoleum. He certainly had a lot in common with him. Walton said how pleased he was to get the site because it was 'where Bessemer proved his widely known steel process'.

Did Walton know something about the site that Bessemer wanted kept quiet? It is probably idle to speculate on what Bessemer was doing at Greenwich. Why did he omit to say anything about it himself?

In the foyer of the linoleum works Walton had displayed a small, or maybe a model, Bessemer convertor and an ingot which he said was the 'first flash' of steel made in a convertor. They remained there for many years and eventually, long after Walton's death, the linoleum works was taken over by Nairns of Kirkaldy.

In due course it was closed down and the convertor and the 'flash' were given to the Science Museum. Some twenty years ago I was told that the Museum was very disbelieving of the provenance of these items. However a photograph of the 'flash' is now on line on Getty images and I am assured that both items are in the Science Museum store at Wroughton, labelled as 'made in Greenwich'.

So – what was Bessemer doing building a works in South London? In the early 1860s he was living in a very grand mansion indeed on Denmark Hill. Perhaps he also thought that a steel works not too far from his home would be useful and tucked away from the prying eyes of his licensees at works in the north.

ALEXANDER THEOPHILUS BLAKELY - DRUGS, GUNS, HARD STEEL AND HIGH FINANCE

There is something else, however, which concerns Bessemer's relationship with Greenwich and with the manufacture of heavy ordnance. When Bessemer was first considering gun manufacture he had sought out the holder of a particularly important patent. This was Alexander Theophilus Blakely, who has been described as '*the most significant British gun designer yet*'.

Blakely, like Bessemer, had been rejected by the military establishment and the Royal Arsenal and no doubt both of them felt aggrieved. In 1859, William Armstrong was appointed as 'Superintendent of the Royal Gun Foundry for Rifled Ordnance' at the Royal Arsenal.

He combined this with his role as owner of a large ordnance manufacturing concern, the Elswick Works in Newcastle. This could be seen by other gun manufacturers as involving a potential conflict of interests.

In 1855 Blakely, who was Irish and an officer in the Royal Artillery, had patented a new way of making guns. Bessemer was impressed with it and later said that 'he must stand as the originator and father of modern built-up artillery'. Bessemer henceforth became Blakely's steel supplier.

Blakely is well known in America where some of his guns are exhibited. For example, in Grant Park, Galena, Illinois a cannon stands on display as ' the Galena Blakely' and projectiles fired from it are shown at the US Military Academy.

This gun, they will tell you, fired the opening salvo of the American Civil War at Fort Sumter in 1861. - It was 'the piece that really worried the beleaguered garrison. It was the sound of the future'. In many American military museums Blakely guns are exhibited and their role in the Civil War stressed.

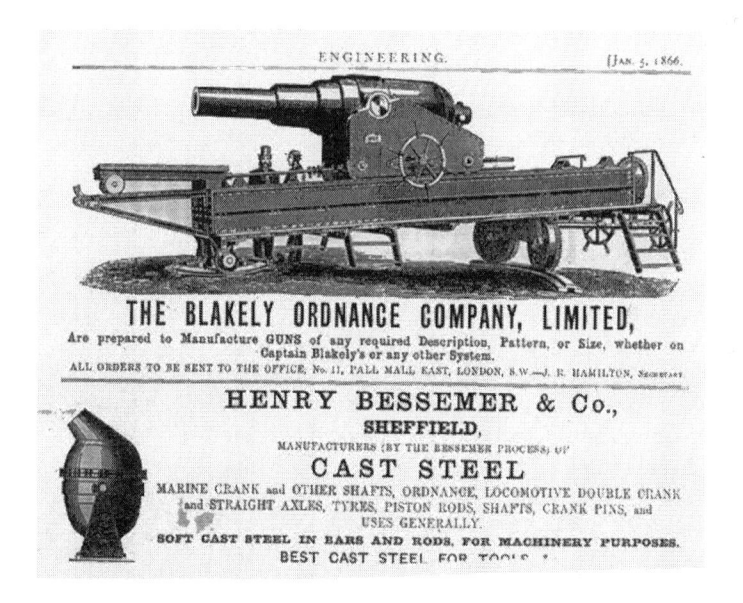

THE BLAKELY ORDNANCE COMPANY, LIMITED,
Are prepared to Manufacture GUNS of any required Description, Pattern, or Size, whether on Captain Blakely's or any other System.
ALL ORDERS TO BE SENT TO THE OFFICE, No. 11, PALL MALL EAST, LONDON, S.W.—J. R. HAMILTON, Secretary

HENRY BESSEMER & Co.,
SHEFFIELD,
MANUFACTURERS (BY THE BESSEMER PROCESS) OF
CAST STEEL
MARINE CRANK and OTHER SHAFTS, ORDNANCE, LOCOMOTIVE DOUBLE CRANK and STRAIGHT AXLES, TYRES, PISTON RODS, SHAFTS, CRANK PINS, and USES GENERALLY.
SOFT CAST STEEL IN BARS AND RODS, FOR MACHINERY PURPOSES.
BEST CAST STEEL FOR TOOLS

Blakely's guns, however, were all made in Liverpool because Blakely did not have his own manufacturing base and guns were made for him at a variety of foundries. In 1863 he said that 400 of his guns had already gone abroad.

It appears that the British Government was not prepared to adopt Blakely's system of manufacture. He thought his guns were required to meet what were said to be unrealistic standards in testing. In 1859 Armstrong gave his patents to the nation and was knighted for his efforts. There has been more than a suggestion made that these patents incorporated elements of Blakely's designs.

Blakely's original patent concerned 'adding successive jackets or rings of differing hardness's of forged metal to an inner barrel permitted the construction of great guns.'.

Blakely was in contact with Morden College in 1863 and in 1864 signed an agreement with them. Although there is no indication in their records that any of the Trustees had taken an interest in Blakely and his guns it might be noted that Thomas Baring, a trustee in the 1860s, had supported the Confederates - to whom Blakely supplied guns - through Baring's Bank.

In 1865 Morden College gave Blakely permission to build a Wharf on the site of what later became Ordnance Wharf. He discussed his proposals with the Metropolitan Board of Works, who sent their architect, Mr. Vuilliamy, down to inspect the site. Blakely later applied to Quarter Sessions in order to put an official closure on a footpath.

It has been said that "the East Greenwich works were clearly established ... for *finishing* ordnance. There were no foundries on the site for casting metal, no mill for rolling plate and only a single, relatively small, steam hammer .... it was intended .. to be an *assembly* not a manufacturing plant.

However, Blakely, and his still unfinished works, were in financial trouble and the Phoenix Gas Company noted that he was unable to pay for the gas supply they had laid on to the new works.

OPIUM`

Contemporary newspaper reports say that Blakely was financed by a John Dent who sold his holdings in the company in 1865 and then went to China.

The deeds of the Blakely site show that his backer was a Wilkinson Dent. Wilkinson Dent was the brother of Lancelot Dent, the man held ransom by the Chinese at the start of the first Opium War in 1841. The Dent Brothers were opium traders - second only in size to Jardine Matheson, the bankers. For many years the Dent family were involved in the Chancery case on which Dickens may have based the story in *Bleak House*. The collapse of the China House of Dent also led to the collapse of Blakely.

In September 1866 Blakely wrote to Morden College giving his address as 11 Pall Mall East - just off Trafalgar Square, and a prosperous sounding location. At the same time a petition of bankruptcy was being filed against him and a winding up order was announced in July. Meanwhile most of his Greenwich factory remained unused and unfinished.

He died two years later in Peru apparently involved in a scandal concerning a society divorce.

It does not stretch the imagination too much to think that Henry Bessemer built his steel works to supply Blakely with steel for guns and that the idea was to build an arms manufacturing complex at Greenwich and 'The new Ordnance Works was to be part of an inter-connected, riverside industrial complex built on a greenfield site'.

It is more than likely that by the time Bessemer died he no longer wanted to make public his keenness to sell big guns to foreign powers.

When the East Greenwich Works closed there were said to be 100 completed guns left on site together with many tons of associated parts. The half-made guns remained there for many years while the site became the South Metropolitan Gas Company's Ordnance Tar Works. They were used as a feature at the tar works gates and were eventually sold for scrap in the 1970s. Every one of them would now be a valuable collector's item worth a considerable sum.

Any remaining assets of the Blakely business seem to have been taken over by Josiah Vavasseur who re-established the works in Southwark. He eventually merged this business with the Armstrong works at Elswick, joined the Armstrong Board and became a very wealthy man. Armstrong's house, Cragside, is famous and is just outside the small town of Rothbury in Northumberland. It may be a co-incidence that just up Blackwall Lane is an old church hall, now in use by an arts organisation. It is called 'Rothbury Hall' and the foundation stone says it was founded by Josiah Vavasseur

Gate of South Met's Ordnance Tar Works showing scrap Blakely guns used as a decorative feature

SHIP, BOAT AND BARGE BUILDING

The River – London River - is the most important factor in determining the industries of the Greenwich Peninsula. Boats had been built, used and maintained all along the riverside since time immemorial. By the 1860s Lower Thameside 'constituted the greatest shipbuilding area in the world'. However I have to admit that the really important shipyards were mainly on the north of bank.

The construction of vessels divides easily into three different sections. First, boats built largely for River use; Second, ocean going ships, and, third, sailing barges plus lighters and specialist vessels. Sailing barges are in many ways a separate subject, built by specialists and on Greenwich Marsh they were established rather later than the boat and shipbuilders. Ship and boatbuilding sites were very largely at the north end of the peninsula with two particularly important areas. One, known as Bay Wharf, is a Morden College owned site on the west bank. The other is now the area around Dome where a dry-dock was built. There were a scattering of other ship and boat building sites in between.

THE WOODEN NUTMEG

The riverbank area now known as Bay Wharf was owned by Morden College and once known as 'Horseshoe Breach'. It was probably formed by a flood breaking into the sea wall sometime before 1620 and its shape meant that it was ideal for boat building slips. And slips were indeed built when Morden College leased it to an American in 1864 for his National Company for Boat Building by Machinery.

Small boats had been made up and down the River for millennia, but never boats like this! Small boats were needed for many reasons, with as many designs as purposes. Nathan Thompson wanted to build boats, thousands of them, and they had to be all identical to each other – and no-one wanted that.

Thompson came from New York where he had been a marine engineer for the previous nineteen years. In 1859 his boat building system had been examined by the US Navy Department. Their report showed that he had made it possible to cut the time and manpower needed to build small boats - but that all the boats had to be identical.

Four years later Thompson came to England. A visitor to the works described the machinery as 'practical.... expeditious and economical' but, for some reason, also drew attention to the manufacture of wooden nutmegs in New England. A wooden nutmeg is apparently sometimes used to describe someone from Connecticut with dishonest intentions.

There were soon a number of backers for the scheme. Thompson's technique was to invite prominent people to a demonstration and ask them to sign a document to say how impressed they were. Chief of them was Colonel Sykes, MP, Chairman of the East India Company. Soon the Company's prospectus included recommendations from an astonishing number of important people, including two Dukes.

Thompson claimed that 25,000 new small boats were needed every year in Britain and he would supply a quarter of them. He knew that 'a quarter of all the ships' boats built in the United Kingdom were for use in Thames built ships'. He said that since his new works would be surrounded by large shipyards he could not fail to sell his boats. He said that if he only made one fifth of all the boats needed in Great Britain then his Company would make a profit.

His system depended on a series of fourteen machines, all steam driven. Boats were built round a central 'assembling form' which held everything together in the right place. This machinery needed a very large cash investment but he said that labour costs would be only a quarter of that normally required. Cheapness meant that independent fisherman and others without access to large amounts of capital could afford to buy new boats more often.

Thompson set about making Horseshoe Breach fit for use by building a causeway and putting a boom across the bay. He faced the River wall with stone. New buildings were to be 'proper brick built structures' by agreement with Morden College.

National Company for Boat Building works

It would be nice to be able to say that Thompson's automated manufacture methods were a great success but, predictably, the company went out of business in its first year. Thompson disappeared along with his boat building system. He had registered his patents all over the world and it is a matter of speculation where he went next.

Information about Thompson has come from the Mystic Seaport Museum in Connecticut. They were upset, they said, at my drawing attention to wooden nutmegs – I was wrong – Thompson was a 'snake oil merchant'. .

Happily much of the capital Thompson had invested in slips and buildings had turned Bay Wharf into a practical ship building area and that is what it became for the next forty years.

MAUDSLAY, SON AND FIELD

In 1864 a different company took over the new slips and boat yard at Horseshoe Breach. The new occupants were the long established and world famous, Maudslay, Son and Field. Henry Maudslay had been born in Woolwich and trained under Marc Brunel. He is shown on one of the stained glass windows in Woolwich's Public Hall with other local luminaries. His Lambeth works is famous for many engineering innovations, including machine tools and eventually marine engines. Henry Maudslay himself had died in 1831 but the firm continued under his sons and reorganised into Maudslay, Sons and Field in 1833.

The East Greenwich site was fitted up so that work could be transferred from Lambeth. They began to extend the slips to take larger craft and by October they had already built a ship - The Lady Derby.

THE LADY DERBY

On what the Kentish Mercury described as a 'great day for East Greenwich' the first ship was launched in October 1865. This was the Lady Derby - named after the wife of the then Prime Minister. She was a screw collier, purpose built to 'Henwood's patent dynamical principles' for the General Iron Screw Collier Co.', meaning that she was meant to carry coal. A dampener was put on the proceedings when Daniel Fitzpatrick, one of the partners in the firm, died the day before the launch - an event that almost led to its cancellation. It meant however that at the 'sumptuous luncheon', which followed, all toasts were cancelled except 'success to the new ship'. The luncheon was, inevitably, at The

Trafalgar, while skilled artisan staff lunched next door at The Yacht, and labourers at The British Sailor in Hoskins Street.

Fitzpatrick's death was bad luck, and bad luck was to stay with the Maudslay shipyard. As for Lady Derby only twelve years after her launch she floundered and was abandoned at sea north east of Whitby when carrying ballast from Granton to West Hartlepool.

The next two vessels to be launched at Greenwich were naval tank vessels – 'Pelter' in 1867 and 'Despatch' in 1869. They were built for use at the Royal William Victualling Yard at Devonport and used for carrying fresh water to the fleet. The two vessels were to remain in service at Devonport until 1905. Tugs were built at the yard. – Grappler for William Cory, their earliest. Alert was built for Herbert Maudslay himself. There were also probably steam yachts and launches and they also had Maudslay built engines.

Two of the most important ships built at Greenwich do not appear in the engine lists at all, because they were sailing ships. There is no explanation as to why this company renowned worldwide for its marine steam engines, should suddenly enter the competitive market for fast sailing ships.

BLACKADDER

Everyone – if they know just one thing about Greenwich - will know about the Cutty Sark. They know about her speed and that she was built in 1869 in Scotland for John Willis. What very few of them will ever discover is that within sight of Cutty Sark is the yard where her two sisters were built, Halloween and Blackadder, built by Maudslay, Son and Field at their Greenwich shipyard.

The first of the two ships was Blackadder, described by Basil Lubbock as 'Built i' th'eclipse and rigged with curses dark'. Most of what has been written about Blackadder seems to be full of a great deal of gloom and doom, but she survived for over thirty years and set many very fast times.

Blackadder was launched in February 1870. She was built to the highest requirement of Lloyds for an iron ship and had a 'complete East India outfit for a full rigged ship'. As she was fitted out it appeared that there was a real problem in construction, which affected the supports for the masts. A further problem came when Blackadder nearly sunk in her dock in London because of a pipe which was not properly set in place. Blackadder was supposed to be 'unlucky' but this seems to be mainly on account of things which 'nearly' happened – she was usually lucky enough for them to be put right in time.

Lubbuck told the story of her first voyage. Her captain is described as 'senseless' and 'fool headed'. Once in the 'Roaring Forties' and at 'the first bit of a blow' which 'showed that the trouble aloft was very serious' the Captain decided on a 'most foolish and risky manoeuvre'. Luckily the young second mate 'kept his eyes glued on the Blackadder's maintop ... there was a flash of fire aloft'. As the rigging fell from the mast .... the mast fell, bursting the main deck. ... tearing up more planking of the main deck. At the same time, the mizzen mast began to sway ominously... the mizzen fell while the 'rudder began to lift in an ominous manner'. By now the foremast too was 'sagging forward' and the sea was pouring through the holes into the deck and into the hold. They were 2,000 miles from the Cape and 1,500 from Rio and with no chance of help.

Lubbock continues that the captain was 'so unnerved' that he 'disappeared below and was not seen again until late in the day'. The mate dealt with the situation while the carpenter's team secured the hole in the deck. By early afternoon the remaining sail had been removed and two 'jury' masts were in place.

It was decided to head for the Cape. In due course she encountered the 'St Mungo' of Glasgow who tried to approach her 'with the intention of speaking to her' but Blackadder was so fast, even with her makeshift masts, that St. Mungo was unable to catch up with 'the lame duck'.

Lubbock continues with the story of how unlucky she was and goes on to describe various collisions. After 117 days out she returned to London, and the insurance men were waiting for her. The court case went on and on. The underwriters would not pay the claim because the mast had not been properly secured and Willis sued Maudslays.

Blackadder next went to Foochow in 123 days with only one collision. She then went to Sydney. She lost her masts again in a Pacific typhoon while carrying coal into Shanghai. In 1873 anchored near Banguey Island she struck a reef. On her next voyage she 'nearly' killed her new master off the North Foreland. Blackadder is described as a 'mankiller' but what she actually did was to break speed records. In 1872 she set a record between Deal and Shanghai of 95 days and made the same time later from Foochow to London. Blackadder stayed afloat, during some terrible disasters – all of which were dealt with efficiently by her crews – and she was very fast.

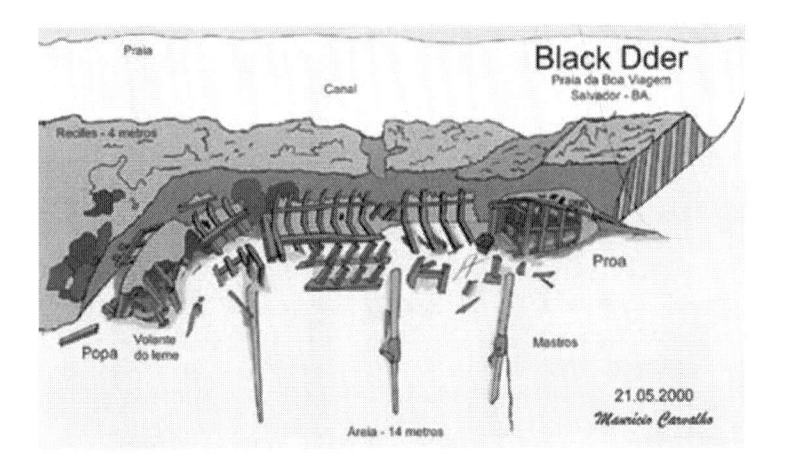

[Diagram: Black Dder wreck plan, Praia da Boa Viagem, Salvador - BA, 21.05.2000, Maurício Carvalho. Labels: Praia, Canal, Recifes - 4 metros, Popa, Volante do leme, Areia - 14 metros, Mastros, Proa]

In 1899 Blackadder was sold to a Norwegian company and in November 1905 she was wrecked at Bahia when entering the port with a cargo of coal from Barry Docks. This might seem to be the end of Blackadder.... and then I received an email from a scuba diver in Bahia.

"One of the sites we visit, especially if we have new divers, is a wreck known locally as the Black Drr, a Norwegian steam/sail ship. Very recently, a local diver has discovered that the ship is actually the Blackadder. She lies alongside the shore line at the bottom of a rock outcrop. Two of the masts lie pointing out to sea and there is very little of her hull left." Divers in Brazil are proud of Blackadder and have produced a plan of her wreck, together with photographs which can be found on their web site.

HALLOWEEN

Blackadder's sister ship was Halloween. She could not be delivered to Willis until the lawsuit was settled and so she sat at Greenwich until she finally sailed in 1871 Lubbock, as usual, can say very little good about her, saying she was docked at Greenwich 'incompetently'. Once on her maiden voyage she got to Sydney in 69 days and she continued with record breaking trips, in particular a journey from Shanghai to London in 91 days. Cutty Sark's best was 110.

She only lasted a few years and was eventually wrecked off the Devon coast, but, like Blackadder, she is not completely gone.

She was on her way to London from Foochow loaded with tea. She had been slowed by bad weather and her crew was exhausted when they saw the Eddystone Light. In huge seas she lost her course and was driven to the shore. At half past seven in the evening she ran into the west end of the Hamstone and crashed at Soar Mill Cove. The crew took to the rigging, and sent up flares. No one saw them. In the morning three men tried to swim ashore but only two of them made it. They reached a farmhouse and the lifeboat reached the ship a few hours later. All nineteen remaining crew were saved and, within three days, the ship had broken up while the cargo of tea washed into Soar Cove where it formed a twelve feet high barrier. The storms covered Halloween with sand and she was forgotten.

In February 1990, Steve Carpenter took his dog for a walk along the beach and to his surprise the previously sandy beach had become all rocks. Storms made diving impossible for some months but eventually a diver went out, and realised that he was above a huge wreck which had appeared in an area they had often dived before. 'Underneath me was a huge hatch, part of a bow and a massive mast lying out across the sand ... you could see the remains of the once proud bowsprit with wood decking all around... and a complete porthole glinting in the sunbeams. Now I knew what heaven was going to be like!'

Most interestingly, the porthole had been made by Stones of Deptford, clearly the subcontractor to Maudslay. Therefore, Halloween now is available to the divers, and another Greenwich built ship is there to be investigated.

THE TURKISH FERRIES

There had been a number of 'Turkish Gentlemen' at the launch of the Lady Derby at Maudslay's yard in Greenwich. It seems that they were there to place orders. It appears from Maudslay's engine list that a number of paddle steamers built for the Bosphorus ferry service had been provided with engines by Maudslay from 1851. Three more names have been unearthed by a paddle steamer enthusiast group – Azimet, Rahat and Selamet. These are said to have been built in London – presumably Greenwich - by Maudslay although nothing more is currently known about them.

The ferry company which provided services across the Bosphorus was called the Sirket-I-Hayriye and since the 1840s had been buying British built ferries. In the late 1860s they had found the need for a different sort of ferry because there was a demand for the carriage of horses, carts, and coaches as well as army transports. Something was needed which could be loaded at each end - a revolutionary concept which was to be worked out by Sirket together with Maudslays.

Sirket-I-Hayriye's manager, Huseyin Haki Efendi, made a rough sketch of the sort of craft, which he needed and he discussed these plans with Iskender Efendi, who had been an inspector for the Turkish Government, and Mehmed Usta, chief naval architect at the Haskoy Shipyard. Usta developed the sketch into detailed designs and took them to Maudslay who built two ferries from them.

The first was finished in 1872 but built for river transport it had to be transported to Turkey under its own steam from London via the Atlantic. In due course she arrived in Istanbul in good order and was named 'Suhulet' which means 'to be easy'.

Suhulet had been designed to carry vehicles and when she was put into service the Bosphorus boatmen protested because they would lose trade. They intended to stop her first voyage from Uskudar to Kabatas but this protest was effectively stopped by the actions of Huseyin Haki Effendi who arranged that the first passengers should be an artillery battery.

The Turkish authorities were so pleased with Suhulet that they returned to Maudslays for a second more powerful double ended ferry. She was to be called Sahilbent which means 'linking two shores' and was named by the Turkish poet, Nakik Kemal

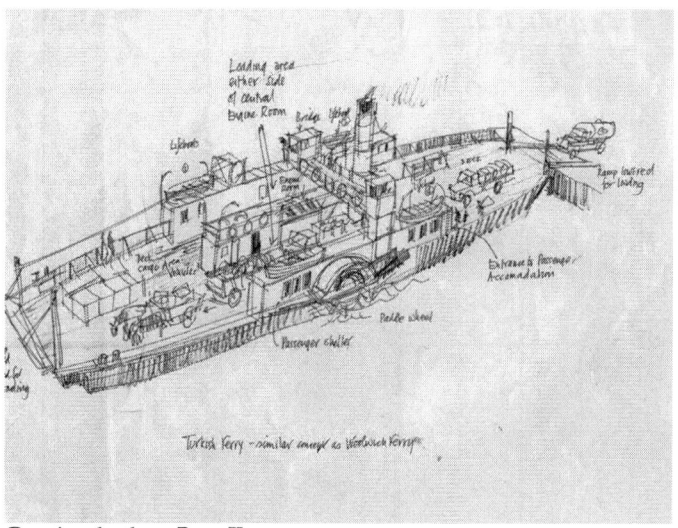

Drawing thanks to Peter Kent

The years went by and Sirket-I-Hayriye was taken into state control and became part of the Turkish Maritime Lines. Suhulet had already been fitted with a diesel engine in 1930 and had lost her tall funnel. In 1952 she was given yet another new engine and some more modifications were made. Six years later after 86 years of work, she was withdrawn from service and broken up for scrap in 1961. Sahilbent, however, continued.

Sahilbent had been first overhauled in 1927 and was taken out of ferry service in 1959 after 87 years of work. She was still seaworthy and so was sold in 1967 and renamed the 'Kaptan Sukru'. Around that time a magazine article is said to have named her as the 'oldest ship still in service in the world. Sahilbent was fitted with a new engine and still appeared in the shipping registers in 1996.

It has not proved possible as yet to discover the current whereabouts of Sahilbent. In 1998 a news agency in Anatolia released a story which was later repeated on the Turkish Pilots service web site. This told how a small cargo ship had caught fire offshore in Pazar County, Rize Province, and had then run aground on the Ardasen Coast. She had left Rize Port with a load of heavy logs to take to a mine at Hopa. The seven member crew were taken off and the ship left to burn. So is this Sahilbent and where is she now? Neither the Turkish pilot service nor the Anatolian News Agency answers our emails. Is she a burnt out hulk somewhere on Ardesen coast? Has she been broken up? – or has she been refitted and refloated? Somewhere in Turkey, is there a boat at work which was built 130 years ago in Greenwich?

THE LAST DAYS OF MAUDSLAY, SON AND FIELD IN GREENWICH.

For the period after 1871 it become much more difficult to find out what ships exactly were built at Maudslays Greenwich yard. Certainly the days of innovative shipbuilding seemed to be over and we are left with only a few names.

There was certainly another tank vessel for use at Devonport. This one was called Elizabeth and she remained in use until 1921. There was a steamer of 1,375 tons - the SS Legislator for the Liverpool based Harrison Line. It is also possible that they built yachts. There is some suggestion that a yacht, Marama, was built at Greenwich and engines were provided for a number of yachts after 1870. There was at least one attempt to build a Torpedo boat in 1879. She is recorded as having a brass hull and was 'a very bad sea boat with good engines' which was broken up in 1896. It may be that this comment in fact sums up the Maudslay's yard at Greenwich – the company made wonderful engines, but the ships never quite reached the same standard.

What was the yard like? It stood on nine and half acres with a 350 ft frontage to the Thames with a deep water jetty. There was a wet dock for barges. At the gate there was a lodge, timekeeper's office and urinals. There was a three bay erecting shop, a galvanising shop, a boiler house, a foundry, a machine shop, an engine house and chimney. There were also offices, a designing room, a stable, a typewriting room, and a strong room. Somewhere on site was a Massey patent steam hammer, and radial drilling machine by Whitworth.

What exactly went on in the yard from the early 1870s to the late 1880s? It is said the yard became a boiler works.

In May 1896, the company wrote to Morden College, the ground landlords, saying that they wanted to extend the lease beyond its expiry date in 1898. They also said they wanted to move Lambeth Works to Greenwich and, again, to extinguish the right of way on the riverside path.

Herbert Maudslay was supposed to negotiate but he cancelled a meeting with Morden College on the grounds that he had to go to Cowes for the yachting. This definition of 'urgent business' explains a lot about the way the company was going. Thirty years previously Herbert had been the owner of Sphinx, said to be the originator of the spinnaker sail, and in 1893 he had founded the Sea View Sailing Club on the Isle of Wight. He remained as Commodore of the Club until his death in 1926.

Did the Maudslay family lose all interest in the Greenwich yard for twenty five years? Perhaps the imminent expiry of the lease was not the only thing which led them to consider the future of the yard. In the 1890s the Blackwall Tunnel was being built almost underneath their site and the Prince of Wales was to open it. Clearly, Maudslay wanted the works to look presentable for the Prince. They submitted a drawing to Morden College of a proposed new gatehouse and it is only this drawing which gives us any clues as to what the works was doing at the time.

The plans submitted to Morden College show a gate on which is written 'Maudslay Sons and Field Ltd. Belleville Boiler Works'.

These boilers had been produced for marine use by the French Belleville Boiler Company and were developed in the 1880s. They had been installed in French naval vessels and 48 had been ordered by the British Navy in 1892 for the cruisers Powerful and Terrible. However, by 1904 the Navy was replacing them with Babcock and Wilcox equipment. Maudslay had clearly not backed a winner and this is must have been another reason for the demise of the yard.

Meanwhile, the Company concentrated on the Prince of Wales. In 1896 the London County Council altered the line of the frontage of the Blackwall premises, hence the need for the new gatehouse. Agreement on this could not be reached and correspondence between the Council and Maudslay's solicitors became increasingly angry. The LCC erected a fence on their version of the line and Maudslay's took it down. Things were beginning to deteriorate.

In March 1898 the company was summoned by the London County Council on account of a dangerous structure on their site. Responsibility for this had now devolved to Morden College, as the ground landlord, since Maudslay had ceased paying any rent and Morden College's insurers were now involved.

In October 1899 receivers were appointed and it was at Greenwich in June 1902 that the bankruptcy sale was held. Equipment from Lambeth was brought down to Greenwich and the site laid out for the sale

The sale catalogue makes for poignant reading. Here is all the machinery and equipment used by one of the leading engineering companies in the world. The first item is of special significance. It is for the original screw cutting and slide rest lathe and set of stock taps and dies made by Henry Maudslay himself in the early 19th century. It is a piece of machinery which, it is said, changed the world. At the auction sale it was bought by the Science Museum and has been on display there ever since.

On the fourth day the auction turned to the offices with their lino, and the stools covered in 'faulty American cloth', to the square of

blue Axminister carpet and a 'japanned tin purdonium'. There
were books 'Bourne on the Screw Propeller'; coloured prints of
the 'Great Western Steamship'. In addition, there were 14
photographs of machinery. Where are those photographs now?
Second on the auction list, after Henry Maudslay's own
equipment, came 'Camera with Wray Lens' – which was what they
considered their second most valuable piece of equipment.
Wray's works still stands by the Ravensbourne in Ashgrove Road,
Bellingham

Morden College assigned the lease to new occupier, and
Maudslay's were largely forgotten in Greenwich, but the family
continued with their engineering and business interests. In 1901,
the Maudslay Motor Company was set up

Eventually the boat builders were to return to Bay Wharf, as we
will see.

STOCKWELL AND LEWIS

In October 1868 Alfred Lewis and John Stockwell moved into the
site recently vacated by Alexander Blakely. They had an existing
ship building works on Bow Creek where they had built a steam
yacht *'Wolverine'* for Major Brandram, the Rotherhithe and Shad
Thames industrial chemist and also some paddle steamers for the
Great Eastern Railway, and others.

The business had been started by Alfred Lewis who had worked
in the drawing office for Samuda Brothers, at Poplar through the
1850s and then opened his own yard on Bow Creek.

Lewis is said to have designed and constructed the new dry dock
at East Greenwich. Lewis and Stockwell applied to have the
Greenwich riverside footpath blocked off through Ordnance
Wharf and, despite some protest from the Greenwich vestry
about loss of ancient rights, this went ahead - and this was
necessary so that the dry dock could be built. It was to be part of a
ship building yard of about two acres which also contained

punching and rolling sheds, a blacksmiths, saw mills, and other factory buildings. The site covered about 3 acres with a 400-foot frontage on the River. The 400 foot dry-dock could take ships of 2,000 to 3,000 tons and the works employed around 300 men.

Bulli

The company seem to have mainly undertaken ship repair work in Greenwich although we know of some ships which were built there. It is possible that work continued for a while at the Bow shipyard and it is sometimes not possible to know which site was used for which ship. External painting of ships and general repairs were carried out in the dock and Lewis claimed that 'Cape ships' and 'P&P Steamers' were repaired there and had to be done on a 24-hour turn round period.

One repair in the dock was described as replacing the stern post of a large ship that had hit a rock. More delicate work was done on 'gentlemen's yachts' and it was claimed that this included a vessel belonging to W.H.Smith - bookseller and First Lord of the Admiralty.

One ship built at Greenwich was Bulli. She was wrecked, in Tasmania. She was built in 1872 and registered at Sydney, New South Wales, for an Australian coal mining company - the Bulli Company. She was steel hulled with twin compound steam engines which appear to be by Ravenhill, and Salkeld – lettering which has been underwater for over 100 years has apparently proved difficult to read. She was also rigged as a three masted topsail schooner. Bulli was wrecked in 1877 when carrying coal from Newcastle to Launceston – both of these are places in Tasmania. Captain Randall was forced by 'heavy southerly gales' to shelter at Erith Island and struck a rock. She is now a site for leisure divers.

Many more ships may have been built by Stockwell and Lewis and there are hints of steamers for Brazil and of paddle steamers for the Great Eastern Railway. They certainly built iron barges for South Metropolitan Gas Company.

Before 1880 John Stockwell was replaced in the company by Samuel Hyam. Neither Hyam nor Lewis lived in Greenwich. Both came from the Westbourne Grove area of west London. Hyam seems to have been a lawyer used by Lewis to negotiate a price for the site when the South Metropolitan Gas Works was planned to be built on the adjacent site. In this context Hyam claimed that ship repairs would be incompatible with the smell of gas 'the prevailing wind will carry coal dust onto the ships. It would only be injurious so far as the dust is concerned'.

Hyam and Lewis asked for compensation if the gas works was built. In due course and following a House of Lords enquiry, the Gas Company was required to compulsory purchase the dry dock and its associated works in 1882.

THE DRY DOCK AND WHAT HAPPENED TO IT

Having got possession of the dry dock the South Metropolitan Gas Company leased it to a ship repair company, Pascoe and

Wright in 1881. Two years later due to the 'non-opening of the valves the caisson was blown up by the water'. In the consequent inrush of water the ship's bows were forced into the dock end and this section had to be rebuilt in concrete. The damaged vessel was the *Richmond Hill* which was in the dock under repair at the time. Richmond Hill was a new twin screw vessel built in Dumbarton only the previous year. As a result of this accident Pascoe and Wright were unable to pay the rent and left.

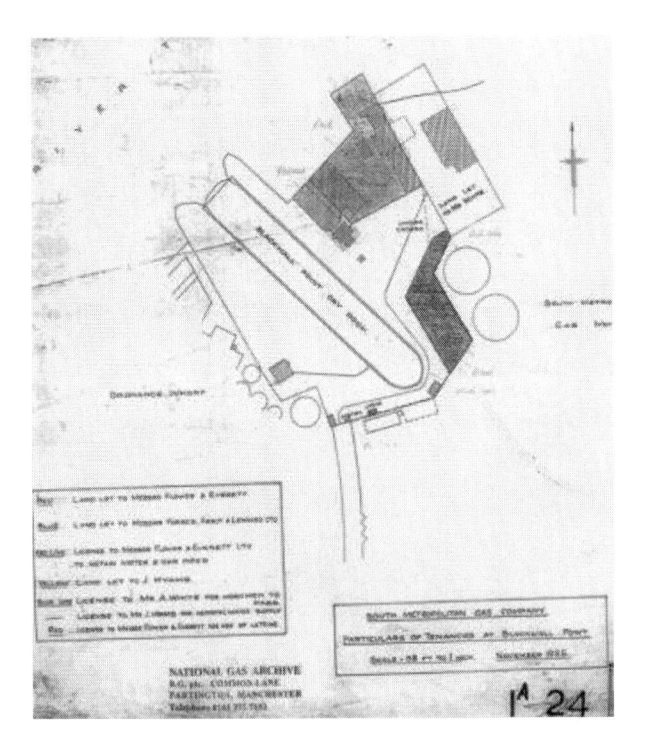

Plan of the dry dock
(Thanks National Grid Archive)

After the *Richmond Hill* incident South Metropolitan Gas Co. rented the dock to the Dry Docks Corporation of London. This was a company set up to amalgamate 28 dry docks on the Thames. Three years later South Met. agreed to arrange a mortgage in order to sell the dock to the Corporation but within a year the Corporation had defaulted on the mortgage and were wound up in 1888. South Met. then decided to dispose of the dock by auction but no bids were received and the gas company was forced to take the dock back and look for a new company to operate it.

JOHN STEWART AND SONS

In 1892 The South Metropolitan Gas Co. began to rent Blackwall Point Dry Dock to John Stewart whose Blackwall ironworks was nearby. They specialised in engines for tugs and steamers. They were a large and successful company with several other sites. The agreement between them was only for three years because the gas company speculated that when the Blackwall Tunnel was built beneath the dock things would change and they could either ask for more rent or dispose of the dock completely. At the end of the three years however they were obliged to relet it at the same rent. In 1900 they finally sold it to Stewarts for £10,000 down and £12,000 in seven years time.

The gas company must have thought they were now rid of the dry dock but by 1910 Stewarts were in financial trouble and the gas company had to buy it back from the liquidators who asked for £21,000 – only £1,000 less than it had been sold for. It then seems to have passed into the ownership of the Port of London Authority from whom the gas company eventually bought it back again in 1925 for £30,000. They turned it into a reservoir, keeping the capstans and some decorative features.

In 1928 the dock caisson was again broken away in a storm but the dock remained in use as a reservoir until it was filled in some time after the Second World War.

A wooden capstan from it remained on the riverside as a commemorative feature for many years and after the gas works closed was discovered mouldering among the long grass and dereliction. It was rescued by the Museum in Docklands where it is now an exhibit.

COURTNEY

There was one other 19th century shipbuilder on Greenwich Marsh although it is very unclear if they ever built any ships.

William Courtney's site was near Ordnance Wharf. He may have had a partner in Mr. Henworth, associated with Maudslay, in the Lady Derby. Although Courtney described himself as a shipbuilder there is no evidence that he ever built any ships, in fact from the archive record, his career lurched from one disaster to another.

Courtney's father was a Surveyor of Shipbuilding for Lloyds and appeared to come from a wealthy Cornish seafaring background. William, born in Padstow, apparently claimed a family relationship with the Earl of Devon. He had been in Newhaven working for a shipbuilder there, called John Gray. When Gray died, Courtney married his widow and thus acquired the assets of the yard. In Blackheath he lived in Lee Terrace and in the early 1860s took on a site in Greenwich Marsh partly owned by Trinity Hospital and partly by Morden College, who, as ever made conditions about construction. Courtney seems to have installed a steam engine, built some 'sheds' and some other buildings but it is unclear if he did anything else. He had ceased to pay rent by 1866 and, in due course, an action for possession was taken against him. He fought the action in the courts and eventual possession by the court sheriff was complicated by the fact that the bailiffs were unable to work out from the boundary markers the exact extent of his land. They reported that it was in a 'disgraceful state'. By the 1870s the remaining debts were written off and a fire finished off any buildings that remained. Courtney himself died in 1875 near Harwich.

This appears to be a straightforward financial failure, but an unexplained incident remains. In 1892, when Courtney had been dead for seventeen years, Morden College recorded that 'Two clergymen' had been in touch 'in regard of settlement of fraud on the Courtney Estate'. This could relate to his marriage, or to his wealthy Cornish relations. Perhaps we will never know.

AND IN THE 20TH CENTURY

Boat building – as distinct from barges - persisted on Greenwich Marsh until as late as the 1980s. A number of firms operated but the final one was Thomas Hughan. They were based at Point Wharf which is the riverside area immediately south of Ordnance Draw Dock, where a theatre is currently being built by Knight Dragon.

Hughan built a series of small boats here throughout the 1960s and 1970s – tugs, launches and so on. Their final vessel appears to have been a replica Mississippi paddle steamer - The Elizabethan - built at Point Wharf in 1971. Elizabethan travels up and down the River all the time operated as a 'party' or 'conference' vessel. I don't know what classifies a vessel as a 'small' boat but Elizabethan must rival in size some of the early 19th century ships built nearby.

The boat building site at Point Wharf remained with rusting equipment until it was removed in the run up to the Millennium Exhibition. It belonged to Joe Jacubaits who had moved there following eviction from the Royal Docks by developers. Joe had moved there after Hughan left. In 1991 he launched the New Orleans – said to be the last passenger boat built on the Thames. Another Mississippi style launch for 100 passengers, she is now based upriver at Henley. At Point Wharf Joe built boats on a special – if makeshift – structure constructed so as to allow pedestrians past.

Bay Wharf is now home to Thamescraft Dry Docking. They are in a boat yard purpose built for them by Morden College as part of the planning agreement for their previous yard at Badcock's

Wharf, now developed for housing. They undertake a wide range of services for river craft, including repairs.

Thomas W. Hughan & Co. Ltd.

Barge and Tug Repairers

Marine Installations and Overhauls

Marine Surveyors and Barge Owners

Floating Dock for vessels 110 ft.

Grid facilities for vessels 120 ft.

Excellent berthing facilities

Engine maintenance and repairs anywhere in U.K.

POINT WHARF, S.E.10

Telephone: GRE 0654—4589
Night: ELT 4562

SAILING BARGES

Boat building - small boats, barges and lighters - has never really left the London River, despite a late 19th century move of most of the industry to the north of England and Scotland. The construction of Thames working boats continued up to the middle of the 20th century – and in particular that of the ubiquitous unpowered Thames lighters and barges. The last to go seem to have been party boats – also essentially working boats.

East Greenwich had never been famous for shipbuilding. Ironically it was after the big ships the rest of the riverside left that boat building here came into its own. For several years at the start of the 20th century a number of prize winning sailing barges were built here which went on to gain many admirers.

There were several barge builders on the Peninsula before 1880 but little is known about them. In the 1800s barges were very common. Every factory and works needed them because they were the main means of haulage on the River and as common as lorries are now. Barge repairers must have had a lot in common with motor repairers – dirty, unglamorous and with a bad reputation. They fitted into the holes and corners which others left and undertook a trade which everyone needed and at the same time disregarded.

The most famous barges were the red sailed bulk haulage carriers of the Thames tideway and beyond, called 'sprit sail' because of the special arrangement of mast and sail which allowed them to be worked with a minimal crew. Bob Roberts, a well known authority on them, described his moment of conversion when he saw Reminder – 'a grey steel barge, gawky and awkward' leaving the Albert Dock with 'a fluttering of white canvas and within a matter of moments she was a cloud of sail'. 'Reminder' is still in sail and berthed at Maldon.

River workers and bargemen lived in a world that was a rather different shape to that of landsmen. They went up river to Brentford and then down to the Estuary, up the coast and well beyond. It was a closed, rather elite, world. There was the river, and then there was everyone else. The two did not really mix.

The barge trade represented what was important about the commerce on London River. They carried dirty, everyday, cargoes - timber loaded in the Surrey Docks, bricks from Sittingbourne, grain for the mills at Ipswich, cement to everywhere and anywhere, scrap iron from Goole, coal to Wapping, flour to Guernsey and granite road chippings back. The larger vessels could cross the Channel - tar from Aylesford to Dunkirk, 'Spent' oxide from Portsmouth Gas Works to the glassworks at Rouen. They went on and on.

Thames Barge design had evolved over many centuries but was refined during the 19th century so in many ways they were very modern. One barge still in sail in the 1990s, but not Greenwich built – is Xylonite. She was built in 1926 as a bulk acid carrier and named after her owners' main product, the first plastic, Xylonite.

The earliest boat builder recorded on the Greenwich Peninsula is a Mr. Cruden who caused a great deal of nuisance to Morden College for some years. He worked on the foreshore in the area where Charles Holcombe wanted to embank the River for wharves. Cruden was not paying rent, and, did not intend to do so. Holcombe told Morden College and James Soames who had part of the site for his soap works agreed to deal with the problem. The matter went to Maidstone assizes and Cruden left.

Another barge builder from the 1860s was a James West whose barge house was alongside the Sea Witch pub. He was either part of, or next to, a barge yard belonging to George Bullock who also had a 'grid iron for ships' further north, but advertised his services as a ship repairer and timber merchant from an address in Thames Street, Greenwich.

Augustus Edmonds leased part of the Blakely site from Morden College before 1880 for a barge building yard. There must have been much more to Edmonds than appears from the brief note about his tenancy because he was clearly a rich man. In 1868 he had leased a very large and important house, which once stood in Westcombe Hill on the site of the present day Broadbridge Close. There were doubtless others whose names briefly appear, the location of whose sites we do not know, and whose barges have been forgotten.

At least one prize-winning sailing barge, City of London, was built at East Greenwich before James Piper arrived. The annual barge races began in 1862 but the builders of contestant barges are not noted for the first years. 'City of London' had been built in 1880 and came second in the 1881 Topsail class. She won the race in 1887 and was still racing ten years later.

Sailing barges are now a glamorous craft despite their dirty cargoes and daily routines. They have something of the same cachet as tea clippers or the great transatlantic liners! They represent the final moments of working sail during the period when the London River serviced the greatest port in the world. They were largely owned by river haulage companies for whom, through their distinctive style, their red sails and their racing prowess, they provided a living advertisement.

PIPER'S

Piper's Wharf was one of the most famous barge building sites on the River and remained in use into the 21st century. In the early years of the 20th century the Piper family produced a long line of successful barges, some of them built to win the annual barge races. Predominant was 'the famous' Giralda built in 1889 - 'champion of champions'.

James Richard Piper had been apprenticed to a Greenwich ship owner, William Bromley, and then went to work for Mowlem's in Greenwich. After ten years he opened a barge repair business where he began to build barges to his own designs and through hard work built the firm up.

There were problems with his first site because of the movement of the tide and Piper moved as soon as he could to a new wharf, which became known as 'Piper's'. By 1899 he had designed and built the largest 'dumb' barges – lighters which did not have their own means of power. His sailing barges too were becoming well known and his order book was full. Piper's had some pretensions above the usual barge and lighter repairers of East Greenwich – advertising themselves from the first as 'Barge and Yacht builders'. In due course other family members took the business over. While they built a wide range of working Thames boats and some pleasure craft they were rightly most famous for their classic sailing barges.

The earliest barge built at Greenwich by Piper was called, fittingly, James Piper - she ended her days as a Chelsea houseboat. She was followed by many others including *Haughty Belle*, *Gerty* and *Ernest Piper*. The remains of many barges can still be seen sitting on Medway mud at Bedlam's Bottom, near Sittingbourne. In the early 1900s Piper's were turning out at least one barge a year. These were commissioned, or sold to the river haulage companies.

Haulage firm Goldsmith's of Grays commissioned *Giralda*. '*Ugly and flat-bottomed*', she was designed to win the prize money for Queen Victoria's Jubilee Year gold cup. She followed this by winning race after race for many years. She had less success as a working barge and coping with the cement, bricks, rubbish or corn - the routine loads of any working barge. Piper's followed with many other barges and most of them led useful working lives. They still aspired to racing success - a barge of 1904 was called *Surge* (*S*ure yo*U* a*R*e *G*iralda's *E*qual). By the 1930s the annual championships were dominated by East Greenwich barges.

Sailing barge careers and their final fates are recorded in detail by the enthusiasts who follow them today. Some Greenwich barges still remain useful, although there is no Piper barge still sailing. *Leonard Piper* was until recently a houseboat at Chiswick, but now broken up, and *Wilfred* is a Victoria Embankment wine bar.

Piper's built many other vessels at East Greenwich – lighters, motor barges and even some launches. In the Second World War they turned out landing craft and 'things of that nature'. For a while, in the 1950s, they specialised in refrigerated craft. They did conversions, for example in 1981 they converted a 3,000 ton vessel for cable repairers in New Zealand.

Leonard Piper at Chiswick Mall
(Thanks to the late David Wood)

The Company kept alive memories of the sailing barges and for many years the great main mast of *Genesta* stood outside the Greenwich works, as a memento. Pipers Wharf is now all modern flats – named by sales staff who know nothing of the history of the site and would be faintly patronising to anyone who mentioned that it would have been nice to have named the flats after the barges built there.

Pipers and their prize winning barges are all gone. The boat repair yard which succeeded them on Pipers and Badcocks wharves moved out as the developers moved in. The foreshore and river wall were declared dangerous and in need of rebuilding. So, the barge stands on the foreshore were cleared away along with the masts of old barges laid along the edge of the riverside path to hold it together – and also to remember the barges they came from.

SHRUBSALL

Shrubsall was another Greenwich barge builder. They were an established company with a yard at Ipswich, at Limehouse and also at Sittingbourne. Then, in 1900 Horace Shrubsall rented a piece of land from Morden College, part of the area which was to be later used by the Delta Metal Co. Shrubsall later took over what was to be known as Tunnel Wharf. This area is now all being developed by Knight Dragon as a leisure area and flats.

Shrubsall were established barge builders when they came to Greenwich, with a good record of producing effective boats. Their barges were soon to challenge Piper's and in the 1907 race

Veronica was only two minutes behind *Giralda*. *Veronica* is now lying on the mud at Bedlam's Bottom with all her ribs showing – but her bow boards were preserved in the, now closed, Dolphin Yard Museum at Sittingbourne. No Greenwich built Shrubsall barge remains active. *Vicunia* was burnt out at Maldon only in 1994 and *Verona* is said to be in use as a houseboat in Stockholm.

The barge fraternity was proud of its record in the Second World War. Several went over for the Dunkirk landings. *Duchess* for example was abandoned off Dunkirk in June 1940. *Valonia* too was lost – and had been discharging tar from Aylesford at Dunkirk when, as her skipper is reported to have said, 'Gerry got there first'.

NORTON'S

In the late 1990s odd bits of plank and chain from Norton's Yard could still be found on the foreshore. Old men from Greenwich Yacht Club would say - '*they were from Dick Norton's ….pick up the barge nails*' - all that is left of a skilled and flourishing trade. Norton's lasted into the 1970s and although Dick Norton sold the yard in 1966 he still came down to visit it. The yard housed an attractive jumble of old sheds minded by Fred the watchman.

Norton's built sailing barges on the foreshore near where the Ecology Centre now stands. A plan of the riverfront, drawn up for the adjacent steel works, shows three Nortons – 'R. Norton, Snr' – 'Norton Bros.' and 'Norton Jnr'. None had a wharf but existed on the foreshore with barge blocks running parallel to the bank. 'R.Norton' alone had a small area inland. Pat O'Driscoll remembered '*There was a little wicket gate in the corrugated iron fence….. Norton had two sheds on the other side, one was for storing tools, nuts, bolts, paint, etc. The other was Fred's living quarters'.*

Verona

In 1908 they rebuilt the wrecked *Empress* as *Scudo* and then built *Scout, Scud* and *Serb* from new. *Scud* was a 64-ton vessel, which worked for seventy-three years until she was broken up in Sittingbourne, only in 1980. *Serb*, bigger at 75 tons had a shorter life of only thirty-eight years before she was sunk off the North Foreland in 1954.

BAY WHARF

Thamescraft, boat repair and dry docking business which was based at Pipers and Badcock's wharves, was moved as part of a planning agreement to Bay Wharf. There were existing barge building slips there built for Humphrey and Grey. In 1908 a Mr. Humphrey had joined several other barge builders at Point Wharf. By 1919 he was in partnership with Mr. Grey, Jnr. and then moved to Bay Wharf where the slips were built. Thomas Hughan replaced him at Point Wharf and remained there until the 1970s.

THE LAST GREENWICH BUILT BARGE IN SAIL

One Greenwich built barge remains in sail – *Orinoco*. She appears to be the only barge built by Hughes & Co. Frederick Hughes had been apprenticed to Greenwich barge builder Augustus Edmunds in 1863. By 1887, Frederick's father, also Frederick, was registered as a barge builder leasing Providence Wharf from Morden College. This wharf was on the site which is now The River Gardens flats with an entrance at the bottom end of Banning Street. Young Frederick lived just round the corner in Commerel Street and later moved to Glenister Road. After the death in 1907 of the founder of the works, the older Frederick, the firm had changed and developed into Tilbury Contracting and Dredging. This firm in due course became the current multinational, Interserve

Hughes built *Orinoco* in 1895, commissioned for Mason's cement carrying fleet based at Waldringfield on the Deben. Records say she was sunk in a collision in the Thames in the 1950s and raised and bought by Laurie Tester of Greenhithe Lighterage Co., restored and then rerigged at Faversham. Since then she has been in a number of hands as a leisure vessel.

BARGES

Barge and boat building has been very tenacious at East Greenwich. So resilient was this industry that the Barge Builders Union continued to meet in Greenwich until the early 1980s. I doubt they have completely gone away.

Of all the industries of Greenwich Marsh boat building seems to be the least likely to have gone forever. It would never surprise me to see something taking shape under cover at Bay Wharf, or perhaps up at the Yacht Club.

Use of an adze at Pipers

STONE AND BRICKS AND CEMENT

All the activity in building factories, workshops and housing used a lot of bricks and cement. Despite the marshy nature of the local land there was a trade in imported stone. Artificial stone was also developed and made here. Cement manufacture was also to play a big part in the Peninsula's industry - and one which must have caused an enormous pollution problem.

THE FIRST BRICKS

Thomas Taylor is the earliest recorded brick maker on Greenwich Marsh. He had been George Russell's foreman at the brickworks on the site which preceded the Tide Mill at the end of Marsh Lane in what later became Riverway. It was Taylor who had incited his colleague, Mr. Bignall, to throw, Philip Sharpe, the Wall Reeve, into the River in 1796.

Thomas Taylor is listed as a landowner 'on the Level' from about 1800, 'land in Pear Tree Marsh'. Six years later he was a subtenant of George Moore, apparently at Horseshoe Breach. The investment there was made jointly with Thomas Tickner, landlord of the Noah's Ark pub, Deptford, and they were still there in 1818. Taylor is said then to have been living at 'Bank Place, Greenwich', and this could be the unidentified building which may have preceded East Lodge, on the Riverside, near the Pilot.

WINKFIELD BELL

The earliest cement works on the Peninsula appears to be that of Winkfield Bell. From 1852, Henry Reid and John Winkfield made Roman Cement on land leased from Holcombe on a site to the north of Morden Wharf Road with river frontage on Morden Wharf. They operated five bottle kilns here.

In 1856, Winkfield, who had been declared bankrupt in 1854, left the partnership and set up a Portland cement works on the opposite side of Morden Wharf Lane, on land leased from Holcombe. He was bankrupt again by 1859.

JABEZ HOLLICK

The earliest and perhaps the longest lasting cement works came to Greenwich in 1841.

Cement manufacture had been all round Greenwich, but not actually in it, for several years. Manufacture was concentrated along the Thames and Medway and developments in the early years of the 19th century had transformed it into one of the leading industrial sectors. There were as many manufacturers as there were patents and ideas. Most works, certainly the most famous, were down River around Swanscombe and Greenhithe although there were some cement and stone factories on the Isle of Dogs before 1840.

Jabez Hollick leased a site at Greenwich from Holcombe in 1849. He seems to have had an earlier short lived works on part of the telegraph cable site but also a works at Borstal in the Medway valley (another important area for cement manufacture). In 1849 Hollick gave his address as Warwick Cottages which then stood at the Marsh Lane end of Morden Wharf Road. He later moved somewhere grander, initially Maze Hill, and then 132 Coleraine Road.

His cement works, adjacent to Morden Wharf, had a long river frontage with a loading dock. There was a sail makers shop, a 'bone' store and a 'snowcrete house', perhaps a storehouse or a demonstration building. Three more kilns were later added. The plant came under the control of W. M. Leake of West Thurrock in 1898. A fire in 1898 destroyed the mill building; the works was eventually taken over by the Associated Portland Cement Manufacturers before the First World War and was still in operation by them in 1935 while the wharf remained in use for barges until the 1970s.

Since the industry was mainly concentrated down river, what was the advantage to Hollick of coming so far upstream? Perhaps he wanted to be nearer to the centres of intensive building operations? Most of the downstream works used chalk supplies from nearby pits, the vast scars of which are still a major feature of the Thameside landscape. It is not clear where Hollick's raw materials came from.

ASHBY

George Crowley Ashby was first involved with cement making in Greenwich in 1856 when he went into partnership with Henry Reid on a site leased land from Holcombe immediately north of Hollick's works on what is now Morden Wharf. He replaced John Winkfield in the partnership. The site comprised a chalk mill, five chalk tanks (one very large) and two sets of coke ovens.

The Ashby family were Quakers, based in Staines where they were major industrialists in the town. George's father, William had been involved in the family bank and had a barge haulage business dealing in building materials. He also made Roman Cement in Staines. Why did the Ashbys come to Greenwich to make cement? It may be relevant that George's middle name was 'Crowley' – implying a link with the Quaker ironfounders who had, for a while, been based in Greenwich.

The company name was changed to the East Greenwich Portland Cement Company once Ashby was involved and, in 1870, it was again changed to William Ashby and Son.

George Ashby died in 1893 and is buried in the Friends' Burial Ground in Staines but the works continued in production. By 1919 it could produce over 410 tons of cement per week. Cement production finally ended in 1926. In 1928, Morden College recorded that the site contained '15 disused cement kilns and 6 chimneys which even if repaired would be an encumbrance to leasing the site'. However the site continued in use by Ashby's for movement of building materials until the Second World War.

AND OTHERS

Henry Reid also had a cement works on part of Holcombe's holding where there were kilns, a dwelling house, a garden, and a boiler and engine house. It seems to have lasted less than ten years.

William Angerstein, the local landowner, also had a short-lived cement works for a while.

COMPOSITION

The word 'Composition' is used to describe a variety of products and can mean a number of things like '*a new paving composition ... pebbles in pitch*' or '*composition for sheathing, preserving etc. ships bottoms*'. The related "*Compo*" can mean anything from an unreliable mortar to a rubbery constituent of cricket balls. An 1826 recipe described a mixture of oil of turpentine and coal tar mixed with resin, size and ochre. More likely what was being made on the Greenwich Peninsula in the 1850s was something like James Wyatt's 1790s invention, "*compo-cement*", designed to be used for stucco.

SIR JOHN SCOTT LILLIE

Sir John Scott Lillie was a retired army officer who owned land in Fulham and began development there from 1826 – hence a number if 'Lillie' names in the area. He was also prolific inventor and held a number of patents, including one, taken out in 1851, for road coverings.

His Greenwich '*composition works*' was probably set up in connection with this. In 1858 he signed an agreement with Willis and Wright, which must mean he had a site at Bay Wharf and in 1859 he built a jetty there. His works is described as a 'factory for the manufacture of composition' with a wharf and jetty. dwelling house, steam engine and chimney shaft. This factory appears in records in the early 1860s but Sir John died in 1868 and the fate of his works is not known.

WILLIAM BUCKWELL

William Buckwell's factory was yet another cement-type works on the northern part of the Enderby site. It was a '*composition works*' but it appears on some 1860s maps as '*old concrete works*'. Buckwell held a number of patents, taken out during the 1840s, for making pipes '*artificially in moulds*' and '*compressing fuel*' which implies the manufacture of briquettes (usually a mixture of coal dust and tar). He also held patents for both scaffolding and steam engines. He patented 'Buckwell's Granetic [sic] Breccia Stone'; this was apparently made of natural stone chippings and Portland cement, formed into slabs under hydraulic pressure.

There are scant details about Buckwell's Greenwich Phoenix Stone Works but rather more drama about his departure from the business world. He is said to have been a railway contractor as well as a manufacturer of artificial stone. Neither occupation can have been much of a success because in 1862 he disappeared. This was because he owed £90,000 - £50,000 of it to Italian creditors. He had been involved in the construction of a railway between Novara and Lake Orta, north west of Milan.

When Buckwell failed to turn up at a bankruptcy hearing in London, Mr. Haydon, of the City Detectives, went to Turin to look for him. He was found at Borgomanero, on the line of his railway '*concealed between the ceiling and roof of an outbuilding*'. Haydon wanted to take him back to London but, of course, his Italian creditors wanted him to stay in Italy. The Italian authorities took him to the frontier with France at the top of Mount Cenis but Haydon was tipped off and got there first. The Italian police escort refused to hand Buckwell over to Haydon but inadvertently crossed the frontier by a few feet (everyone was knee deep in snow). Buckwell was arrested by French police who said they would shoot him if he tried to escape back to Italy. Meanwhile the Italian soldiers refused to leave unless they could take him back to Turin. It was a very long and very cold night and the discussions were protracted but Buckwell was returned to London and gaol.

GRANITE WHARF – REAL STONE

Real stone was imported into Greenwich through one of the first wharves to be opened on the Marsh. This was the second site developed by Coles Child and was later taken up by the highway contractors Mowlem.

The original John Mowlem had been a worker in the Dorset stone quarries who came to London to find work with a sculptor. He founded the contracting firm in 1823 beginning with paving contracts and a wharf at Paddington. By 1852, he himself had retired back to Swanage and the firm was managed by his nephew, George Burt. Between them Mowlem and Burt managed to take back to Dorset an extraordinary collection of bits and pieces of street furniture from London which can be seen re-erected in the seaside town.

Mowlem's main yard was at Millbank and the Greenwich wharf is described as their 'stone yard' and no doubt many of the items now in Swanage were taken to Greenwich before being shipped out. In the early 1860s 'Mowlem are building substantial buildings on their site'. By 1869 there were two tracks of rails going towards the River, there was a slip, 'mooring posts' and a crane.

We would know almost nothing about Granite Wharf if it were not for one picture which is sold at The Durleston Country Park near Swanage as a postcard. The picture shows the Great Globe, now at Durlston Head, under construction in Greenwich. Two stone carvers sit on top; behind it is a great crane – perhaps the one shown on the map – and in front are three figures. One has been named as John Mowlem Burt, George Burt's son.

Mary and Naz Wright 1947

The Globe seems to have been the idea of George Burt who, a few years earlier, had commissioned a smaller granite globe which is now on display in Beaulieu. The Great Globe is made of 15 pieces of Portland stone held together with granite dowels. It was taken from Greenwich to Swanage in sections on one of Mowlem's sailing vessels and erected at Durlston by a Dorset builder. Whether the stone was taken originally from Swanage to Greenwich for carving is not known – but the expense of carting 40 tons of stone between the two must have been considerable.

A roadway along the western boundary of the site ran from what was then Chester Street (now Banning Street) to the River. This was called 'Paddock Place' and later Cadet Place and was obliterated by the current housing development. A wall here was extraordinary, consisting of what appears to be pieces of random stone, some of it set up as a sort of blocked up gateway. Geologists were interested in it, dubbing it 'Cyclopean'. The stone has been identified as part of the stockpile of stone which Mowlem's had in the yard.

It is thought that stone quarried in Dorset was shipped to Greenwich to be held here until it was needed elsewhere. It would then be transhipped by Thames barge. It includes, says geologist, Eric Robinson: 'White Portland Stone, some of it dressed with the stone pick, pink and red sandstone – not necessarily as hard as the coal measures York Stone .... they are joined by 'Bluestone' (Diorite) ... at either side the blocks sit at unusual angles with an infill of angular pieces of dark bluestone – this dark stone came from Guernsey in the Channel Islands and was much used in kerbs and cobbles'. It is pointed out this miscellany of stone pieces might serve as a museum of the sort of stones which made up the stone cartage trade in the English Channel. 'Just add some granites' he continues 'look at the cobbles and smaller cube setts in the entrance to the yard and you see all of these granitic rocks polished by cart wheels and cars'.

When the current housing was planned local people asked for this random stone wall to be preserved and rebuilt. This happened but in the rebuilding the masons working for the developer squared it all up neat and tidy so the preserved wall might well be random stone but it is nothing whatever like what was supposed to be preserved. You need to go to Watchet Station to see what it used to be like - Eric Robinson had a replica built there.

PATENT STONE – STONE MANUFACTURED IN GREENWICH

In 1866 Frederick Ransome came from Ipswich to take over a site roughly on the area of today's Victoria Wharf for a '*patent stone works*'. He described this as an '*immense factory…on an ugly and pestiferous marsh*'. It is perhaps noteworthy that the site was partly owned by Henry Bessemer, the steel magnate.

By 1868 Ransome was in business with a counting house, chimney, wharf, jetty and so on. The stone making process was somewhat complicated but in essence the idea was to '*dissolve common flint*' and turn it into '*glue*'. This was used to bind pure sandstone with cement of silicate of lime. The result could be worked in a plastic state and later with a chisel like natural stone. It was said to produce '*carvings like the best Portland stone*'. Some of Ransome's concrete can be seen at St.Thomas's Hospital in London.

The factory manager was his son, Ernest Leslie Ransome who lived in Royal Hill Place with his wife, Mary, and two children. He was one of the agricultural implement manufacturing family and had become interested in making artificial stoneware. This was an important Suffolk industry and a number of leading manufacturers came from there. Several of the Greenwich factory workers had come from Suffolk with Ransome and some lived near the works - including the publican of the Star in the East who came from Walton-on-the-Naze and whose brother-in-law, William Brooks from Mistley, was an architectural draughtsman in the stone works. John Felgate the gatekeeper came from Suffolk.

Some of the stonework made in the Greenwich factory still survives. Anyone who travels to Chester Station will find the company's identification plaque embedded in the ground in front of the exit staircase. In Greenwich some of the company's nameplates can be seen in the pavement of St.John's Park.

The Ransome factory was only short-lived. By 1878 it had been taken over by Hodges and Butler. Ernest Leslie Ransome went to America in 1872 where he founded the Ransome Concrete Co., famous for a cable car system which withstood the 1906 earthquake and for buildings like the 15-storey Ingalls Building in Cincinnati, the world's first reinforced concrete skyscraper in 1903. He is said to have 'devised the most sophisticated concrete structures in the United States at the time'.

HODGES, BUTLER AND DALE

Hodges, Butler and Dale, took over the stone works from Ransome and it is intriguing that the rates were paid in the name of Henry Bessemer, himself as owner. In the future the factory was variously known as 'Thames Silicated Stone or 'Imperial Stone' and the area became known as 'Imperial Wharf'. The company was owned by a James William Butler who lived in Montpelier Vale, Blackheath and John Anderson, a cement manufacturer from Faversham, who was also involved in a works at Upnor.

PAVING SLABS

A number of works were opened after the Second World War, which specialised in the manufacture of paving slabs. These included The London Phosphate Syndicate, concrete slab manufacturer, W. Rees, concrete slab manufacturer and the Rheocrete Paving Stone Slab Co.

Demolition of East Greenwich No.1 Gasholder 2019- 2020 – interior pictures taken on site visits by GIHS members

COALFIRED POWER

THE GAS WORKS

In the mid 19th century the coal trade was at its height. Ships from the north east of England and Scotland poured into the Thames. Coal came into the wharves on the Peninsula for all sorts of reasons. Some of it was used as a the source of the raw materials for chemical plants, but the main use was to fuel the boilers of the steam engines which began to provide power for the new factories. After 1880 coal was used to supply centralised power plants – like gas works, and later on electrical power stations.

The South Metropolitan Gas Works grew to dominate the Greenwich Peninsula - it was built in the 1880s and was thus a late comer, sited on an area hitherto unused for industrial purposes. It was also very 'modern' – no gas works has been built in London since. It was the new, 'super', works through which the South Metropolitan Gas Company hoped to show the world what it could do.

GEORGE LIVESEY

George Livesey was the Chairman of the South Metropolitan Gas Co. when the East Greenwich Gas Works was designed and built. He was the dominant figure of the 19th century gas industry, effecting great changes although not without some controversy. His childhood in the Old Kent Road gas works left him with fond memories of local people and those who worked for his father there. He signed the 'pledge' of temperance in his early teens along with a group of other young workers and, through them, began to attend prayer meetings and the London Band of Hope.

Temperance was to become his 'other' career and George maintained a lifetime close association with bodies like the Lord's Day Observance, and the Good Templars. Somewhere along the line he picked up ideas from Christian Socialists, co-operators, and most significantly the Italian patriot, Mazzini.

A gas works may not seem the best ground from which to launch a crusade – but George was generally unstoppable. He was clever, good at everything he did, and could never resist a good cause - which ranged from the minutiae of gas works equipment up to grand schemes on the organisation of society itself.

By the 1870s George Livesey (pictured) had moved the gas company on to the national stage. Through his negotiating coups South Metropolitan had taken control of a number of other local gas companies thus gaining a near monopoly in the area. He had got the Government to force private gas companies to peg their dividends so they could only rise if the price of gas went down.

In the 1860s the two biggest gas companies in North London had both built large out-of-town works to provide bulk supply and enable them to close down small uneconomic works. Livesey decided that it was high time South Metropolitan did the same - but better - and in the early 1880s the site on the marsh was chosen.

BUILDING THE GAS WORKS

The new gas works was different to the industries which had already come to the Peninsula. As a large public utility, albeit a private company, it had a direct relationship with Parliament and the local authorities. It was not so concerned with any restrictions that Morden College, or other landlords, might impose, and it was big and powerful enough to impose itself on the area around it.

The Gas Company received Parliamentary permission to build the works in December 1880. Discussions were already underway with the local authority on the new plant and its layout. It had been agreed that the purifying plant, thought to be the smelliest part of the works, should be placed on the northern most tip of Blackwall Point. This would ensure that smells were kept from Greenwich, while wafting over the Isle of Dogs.

There were a number of objections to their plans. Coles Child's executors wanted to build housing, as did Mrs. Fryer, another landowner. Lewis, the owner of the dry dock on Blackwall Point claimed that the smell would damage the high-class paintwork his firm said they were doing. Parliament made some requirements before the works could be built - one was that they rebuild the river wall on the eastern bank, and provide Ordnance Draw Dock. The public footpath round the riverbank was closed.

None of this pleased *'waterside people'* who continued to cause *'difficulty'* by insisting on their old rights of way. Docwra, the gas company's contractors, dealt with this by placing *'a gang of men'* to *'divert this traffic'*. Building work began very slowly. The contractors found access to the site difficult, describing it as *'a cul de sac - and approaches thereto were not inviting'*. Most of the site on which the gas works was to be built, in the centre of the marsh, was *'market gardens of poor quality'*. The builders were constantly reminded of this by the *'sprouting of rhubarb'* throughout the site. Other reminders of the rural past were a few remaining cows which lived in a shed which *'age had rendered rotten and insecure'*. Others who thought they might have rights in the area were those for whom it was a *'happy dumping ground'*. With them the contractors were in a '*constant state of warfare*'. During one such running battle, Joseph Tysoe, the future works manager, only escaped serious injury when his assistant intercepted a heavy iron bar aimed at his head.

As work progressed, Docwra brought on site '*extraordinarily powerful pumping apparatus*' and took borings to discover the state of the ground. Barge after barge came loaded with clinker and heavy rubbish to use as infill, but it took '*a vast amount of effort to make a sensible impression on this wilderness*'.

Slowly the works took shape. '*Looming vast against the sky is the skeleton of the great holder*'. This is the holder to be seen until May 2020 alongside the Blackwall Tunnel approach road. It was thought it would '*darken the sky like a mountain of iron*'. The jetty too was taking shape, sinking as it was built. It was reported that it was '*allowed to go as far as it would*' until it became '*as firm as a rock*'.

East Greenwich gas works became world famous, and was once seen as an example of everything that was progressive in British industry.

THE GASHOLDERS

Ever since the gas works came to the Peninsula in the 1880s the structure which dominates the landscape has been the giant gasholder, East Greenwich No.1. For most of the time an even bigger neighbour stood alongside it. At twelve million cubic feet capacity, East Greenwich No.2 Gasholder was the biggest in the world when it was built in 1892. Two 'flying lifts' gas holder tanks built to rise above the top edge of the framework, were destroyed by the 1917 Silvertown TNT explosion and never replaced. No.1. is (or was) slightly older and smaller – small, in the sense that it was only surpassed by its companion.

George Livesey believed in maximising both economy of construction and greatest storage capacity for ground area. The holders were built without decoration as a symbol of all that was modern and progressive in British industry. The observer was expected to see them and be impressed, not only with their size but with their rationality.

East Greenwich No.1 stood until demolished in June 2020. Thousands of people signed a petition to keep it but authorities beyond Greenwich have decreed it would go.

CHANGE

For George Livesey the works was to be more than just another gas supply factory but was to embody the ideals, which he had cherished from boyhood. Within a few years of its opening a dramatic episode in industrial relations was to change both George Livesey and the South Metropolitan Gas Company in a fundamental manner.

In the late 1880s London was changing. Arguments about the government of London had led to the abolition of the Metropolitan Board of Works and, in late 1889, the election of the first London County Council. Ideas about public ownership of gas were discussed, something which, naturally, Livesey did not approve of.

THE GREAT 'STRIKE' OF 1889

1889 was the year of the Great Dock Strike. There had been trade unions in the gas industry since the 1830s and a bitter dispute in 1872 had led to legislation that made strike action illegal for gas workers. In the late 1880s Will Thorne and others began to organise gas workers, but Livesey was determined that 'outsiders', as he termed the union, should not have any power in 'his' works.

One morning Livesey walked over Telegraph Hill in Nunhead and looked down at the works. He later said that he suddenly knew what to do. He instigated a profit sharing scheme amongst the South Metropolitan workforce. The Gas Workers Union objected because it included an anti-strike clause. They threatened action but, because they were unable to strike without breaking the law, the workforce handed in their notices en masse.

Livesey sealed off the works in a state of siege and marched in 'replacement labour' with the help of professional strike breakers. The new workers came in by rail through Westcombe Park Station and proceeded down Blackwall Lane inside a police cordon, to the jeers of the watching crowd. Fights and scuffles constantly broke out in Blackwall Lane. 'Old' workers held a bonfire party outside The Pilot pub in Riverway where they burnt an effigy of Livesey. The great gasholder was watched constantly because if gas pressure fell then the company would have lost because contracts with local authorities - largely sympathetic to the strikers - would be broken. It did not fall and, in effect, Livesey had won.

CO-PARTNERSHIP

Once the dispute was over Livesey began to expand his scheme. Any worker with ideas about trade unions was best advised to keep them to himself. The profit sharing scheme began to evolve into something that Livesey called 'co-partnership' and a whole structure of participation and involvement began to be built up.

Workers could take grievances to 'Co-partnership Committees' which could also recommend changes in a wide range of working practices. They involved themselves in decisions on the various funds - pensions, sickness and so on, managed by company representatives. Co-partnership committees were elected by the workers with an equal representation from management.

In the 1890s Livesey managed to get the company structure altered by a reluctant Board and House of Commons to allow three board members to be directly elected by the co-partners in the workforce. Livesey was nothing if not thorough.

In the years that followed he lectured and wrote constantly about his system. The other London gas companies found it more useful to keep in with Will Thorne. Livesey gradually moved towards a group of idealists on the fringes of the Co-operative movement, the Labour Co-partnership Association.

In 1906 he was to be National President of the Band of Hope and continued to speak on platforms throughout the country on their behalf and for related causes which continued to provide audiences plus bands, flowers and acclaim. The knighthood - and his place in innumerable worthy causes and on Commissions after 1900 - may well have been as much to do with his temperance works as anything.

EAST GREENWICH WORKS

How did all this affect East Greenwich? Alongside the main gate of the gas works stood the Livesey Institute - a meeting room, hall and theatre. Alongside it was the bowling green, and, in due course a War Memorial. To the south were the allotments and sports facilities.

East Greenwich No.1 Holder. Demolished 2020.

George died in 1908 and his place as Company Chairman was taken by Charles Carpenter. Chemical weapons were later added to the East Greenwich repertoire as the Great War began.

Most of all, of course, there was the showpiece gas works, probably almost the biggest in the world, and certainly the most modern. Every department aiming at nothing less than perfection. Dedicated public service to standards that were not only high but encompassed progress and modernity. If that standard was not always reached it was not for lack of saying so. By the time nationalisation came in the late 1940s the South Metropolitan workforce was proud and exclusive. To be a gas worker in Greenwich was to be something very special – better than any other gas workers - better, in fact, than anyone else.

ORDNANCE TAR WORKS

Pitch bed and stills

The gasworks was fundamentally a huge complex of fuel production plant and several chemical works. On what had been the Blakely gun manufacture site the gas company built Ordnance Wharf, - a huge purpose-built tar factory. Here tar was processed for sale as required – much of it for use on roads, for which the Company also maintained a fleet of specialist tar spreading vehicles. There were experts who could tell the difference between a bewildering range of tars and tar products.

There was an immense and awful pitch bed and storage tanks below ground.

PHOENIX WHARF

Frank Hills died in the 1890s and his two eldest sons also died within a year. Their Greenwich chemical works was sold to the gas company. It was duly modernised and became part of the East Greenwich Gas Works, having been renamed 'Phoenix Wharf'. Gas works waste products had been the staple raw material of Frank Hills' works for fifty years and now the new gas works incorporated it and made it part of their establishment.

The last memory of chemicals at East Greenwich was an amazing 1950s parabolic building used for the storage of sulphate of ammonia. It was demolished in the late 1980s, while under consideration for listing, because, the owners said, illicit 'rave parties' were being held there. You can still see it used as a stage or a backdrop in 'pop' videos and plays of the period, – including most famously, Dr.Who. Film makers loved it!

COLLIER SHIPS

The gas works included an enormous jetty –more or less on the site of the present clipper pier. Quantum Cloud, the art work by Anthony Gormley stands on remains of the original gas works jetty. No electrical power was used in the gas works and the jetty worked entirely on a hydraulic system which was completely silent.

Collier ship Togston

Coal was delivered to the gas works by the Company's own collier fleet from the Northumberland and Durham coal fields. Before the Second World War there were seven vessels- each of 2,000 tons capacity. Four were lost during the war - *Brixton*, which was mined, *Old Charlton*, dive-bombed, *Effra* torpedoed by an E-boat and *Catford* mined.

The fleet after the war consisted of *Camberwell, Redriff, Brockley* and *Effra*. A replacement *Effra* was described in 1946 as the last word in luxury as she entered the Thames with her first cargo of coal from Newcastle. She had what then was all the latest equipment, including an echo sounder.

A rail link from the Angerstein line ran into the works but was apparently only used to send out tankers full of tar.

COALITE

From 1931 the gas company operated under licence a Coalite plant from British Coalite. Coalite is low-temperature coke used as a smokeless fuel. This stood to the south of the works in the area now covered by West Parkside and Memorial Gardens.

FUEL RESEARCH

The Fuel Research Institute was Government owned and stood adjacent to the South Metropolitan Gas works. Its role was the investigation of coal based chemicals and the use of coal as a fuel.

In March 1952 the Duke of Edinburgh, described as *'a good looking young man who drove his large Austin Saloon*' visited the station. They explained to him the wartime smoke elimination process as well as experiments on combustion in vortex chambers. He was shown the Calorimeter building for research in domestic heating, which was unique in the world. The Research buildings were south of the Pilot – possibly in the area covered by the present pub garden.

WAR MEMORIAL

The only thing which remains from the gasworks – apart from some fragments of the gas holders - is the war memorial. This had been erected and dedicated in 1926 standing in a little garden near the entrance to the works. It was saved by Kaye Murch who had worked in the gasworks and by chance ended up as the sole remaining employee when the site was taken over for building the Dome.

Kaye was determined that something must be saved from the gasworks but sadly died before the war memorial could be properly installed in the redevelopment. It now stands in John Harrison Way on land now called 'Memorial Park'.

Recently the new school built nearby the re-sited memorial has undertaken a project about the people listed on it. Kaye would be so pleased.

Gasworks War Memorial

THE GHOST

The ghost of George Livesey is a silly story which I should not repeat in a sensible book. Around 1998 the Guardian newspaper published a double page spread about the proposed Millennium Dome. On a tour round the works the reporter was told, jokingly 'of course there's a ghost here'. Somehow or other I found myself on TV telling people about George Livesey and speculating whether it was his ghost. With the Dome press officer I speculated that Livesey wanted to visit the Dome because one of the exhibition areas reproduced a seaside scene which we thought could have reminded him of holidays he had enjoyed in Eastbourne.

Some years later I met a man who told me he 'was' the ghost. In the Second World War he had been staying overnight in the gas works and wrapped himself a sheet and gone to sleep on the carpet in the director's office. In the morning he confronted, and terrified, the cleaner when he stood up still wrapped in the sheet.

THE END OF THE WORKS

For forty-odd years after the works had closed East Greenwich No.1 - Livesey's great gas holder, 'the mountain of iron' - stood alongside the motorway as the area changed around it.

There had been an abortive application in the mid-1990s to list it as an outstanding relic of past industry and later English Heritage commissioned a report on the gasholders remaining in London. East Greenwich was not included. To cut a long story very very short it appeared it was on a list for demolition and that there could be no challenge to that. A campaign began – a petition was launched which showed how it as valued as an icon for the area. By June 2020 – as I write this text – it has been demolished. A piece of wanton destruction undertaken most probably because of its proximity to the, locally hated, Silvertown Tunnel.

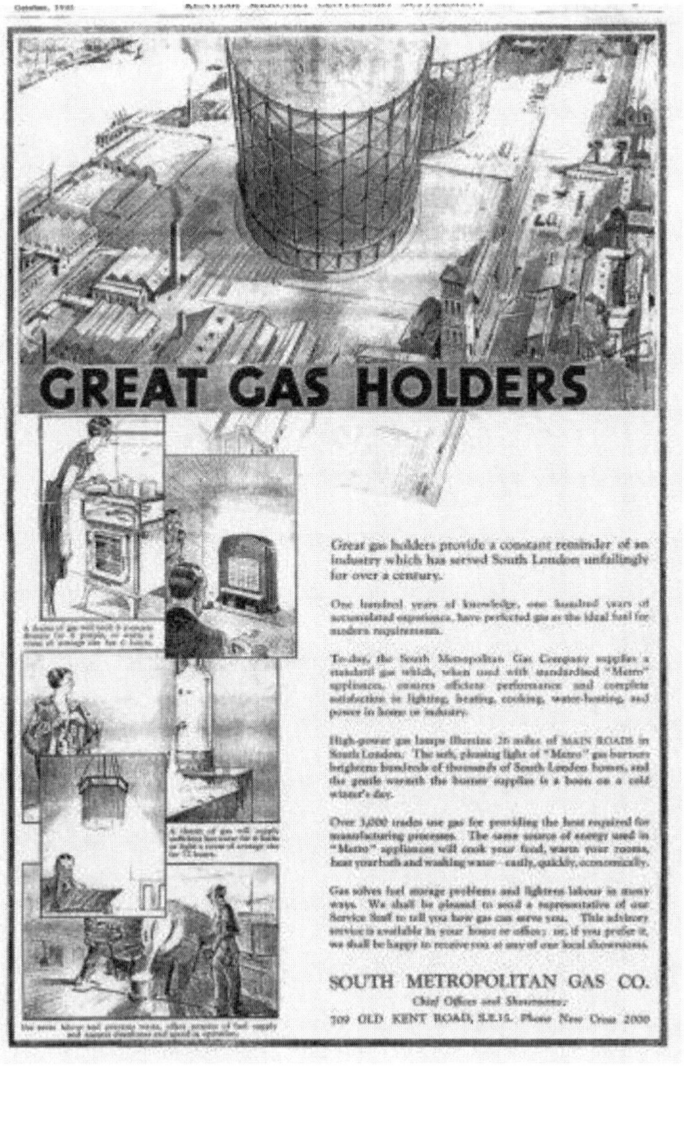
GREAT GAS HOLDERS
Great gas holders provide a constant reminder of an industry which has served South London unfailingly for over a century.
One hundred years of knowledge, one hundred years of accumulated experience, have perfected gas as the ideal fuel for modern requirements.
To-day, the South Metropolitan Gas Company supplies a standard gas which, when used with standardised "Metro" appliances, ensures efficient performance and complete satisfaction in lighting, heating, cooking, water-heating, and power in home or industry.
High-power gas lamps illumine 26 miles of MAIN ROADS in South London. The soft, pleasing light of "Metro" gas burners brightens hundreds of thousands of South London homes, and the gentle warmth the burner supplies is a boon on a cold winter's day.
Over 3,000 trades use gas for providing the heat required for manufacturing processes. The same source of energy used in "Metro" appliances will cook your food, warm your rooms, heat your bath and washing water—easily, quickly, economically.
Gas solves fuel storage problems and lightens labour in many ways. We shall be pleased to send a representative of our Service Staff to tell you how gas can serve you. This advisory service is available in your home or office; or, if you prefer it, we shall be happy to receive you at any of our local showrooms.
SOUTH METROPOLITAN GAS CO.
Chief Offices and Showrooms:
709 OLD KENT ROAD, S.E.15. Phone New Cross 2000

LATE 19TH CENTURY INDUSTRY

As the 19th century drew to a close more and more industries came to Greenwich Marsh. It becomes increasingly difficult to categorise them and there were all sorts of activities and manufactures. Many were clearly existing companies with works elsewhere now looking to move to a large site with water access near London. Here are some of them.

LINSEED - SEED CRUSHING

At some point in the late 1860s or early 1870s a seed crushing mill was set up on the site recently vacated by the bankrupt shipbuilder, William Courtney. It is this mill, which has led some researchers to claim that there was a windmill on the Peninsula. This however was a steam mill and the seed being crushed was almost certainly linseed intended to be used as a source of oil.

The works was originally the 'London Seed Crushing Co.' which became bankrupt. Two more companies involved in seed crushing took over the site and both of them also failed. From 1885 the premises were run as Greig & Co.'s Mills until the late 1890s.

ASBESTOS

In 1898 the Greig's oil mills site was let to Bell's Asbestos Company Ltd with Poyle Mills Company Ltd as sub-tenants. Bell's were based in Southwark Street – the doorway to what were their offices still shows their 'Bell' motif - having originated with John Bell. They were manufacturers of asbestos for steam engines and electric machines and used Canadian deposits of asbestos. In 1909 they moved production from Greenwich to Harefield.

SOAP

The Thames Soap Works, on the site of what became the Amylum sugar works, was owned by a company called Wilkie and Soames. In the early 19th century London soap makers were taking advantage of new manufacturing processes as well as having access to oil from South Seas whaling and products of colonial exploitation, like coconuts.

The Soames family had a soap works in Wheeler Street, Spitalfields, from 1809 but their original partner, Mr Wilkie, had died in 1821. Their Spitalfields works was the tenth largest soap works in the country but they needed somewhere to expand and thus moved to Greenwich.

WILKIE & SOAMES' CELEBRATED COLD WATER SOAP.

THIS SOAP IS PERFECTLY PURE, NO WASHING POWDER OR OTHER MIXTURE INJURIOUS TO CLOTHES IS REQUIRED. Washes equally well in Hot or Cold Water

MADE ONLY BY WILKIE & SOAMES, GREENWICH. BEWARE OF WORTHLESS IMITATIONS.

WILL DO MORE WORK IN THE WASH TUB WITH LESS LABOUR THAN ANY OTHER SOAP. THE PERFECTION OF SOAP.

The Soames family were Greenwich residents. James Soames had lived in the Red House in Maze Hill since 1849 and the family were active in Greenwich life. William Aldwin Soames was Vicar of Greenwich and James Soames, Jnr., paid for the building of St. George's Church in Westcombe Park, where the living went to another brother, Henry Kolle Soames. In local politics, Walter Soames was Mayor of Greenwich before the First World War and his daughter, Olave, was to become internationally known by marrying Baden-Powell.

Most local factory owners were content to let local events take their course, to use the workforce and its skills, and move on but the Soames lived locally and tried to get the community into their way of thinking – Church of England and Liberal.

James Soames approached Morden College Trustees for an underlease on part of the Holcombe site. They had already had numerous dealings with the Rev. William Soames on local charitable causes, including the construction of Christ Church, East Greenwich, and expected high standards from such an important local family. When bricks for building the soap works were made on site the College waived the usual royalties.

The Thames Steam Soap Works employed more than 140 men and boys and James Soames boasted that he contributed to good works in the neighbourhood from the money he made. In 1864 there were special departments for glycerine and paraffin as well as soap boiling and candle making. There was a laboratory, stables and maintenance department, separate toilets and canteens for men and women workers and housing for the gatekeeper and housekeeper. The company's slogan was '*Greenwich the world standard in both soap and time*'.

The soaps included '*Apron*', '*Big Wilkie*', '*Spry*', '*Wonderful Washer*' and '*British Carbolic*' - no-nonsense, heavy-duty cleansers for the hardworking housewife in her war against dirt and disease. Carbolic soap is of course made using coal tar derived chemicals and we need to remember that in this period coal tar was not seen as dangerous but as a useful germ killer.

Towards the end of the 19th century giant soap companies from the north of England threatened the older London industry. Wilkie and Soames fought off take-over bids from 1902 onwards but were eventually swallowed up by Unilever who closed the Greenwich factory in the 1930s. Some traces of the old soap works remained inside the Amylum factory where a couple of old walls - much shored up - still advertised Thames Soap Works. They were destroyed by the French demolition team which pulled down the Amylum plant with no reference to any local organisation before they did so.

FORBES ABBOTT

James Forbes and John Abbott were specialists in ammonia and tar based products. Forbes and Abbott were based at '*very large works*' at Iceland Wharf, Old Ford, in Hackney from the mid-1840s processing waste ammonia bought from the gas industry. They expanded to East Greenwich where they made a variety of chemical products including anthracene and hydrochloric acid. In 1889 South Met Gas took over their site at Ordnance Wharf and they moved to Sussex Wharf, between the tar paving factory and the old Ransome stone works. They also had works at Shoreham and Rye in Sussex and later became the Standard Ammonia Co.

The Forbes Abbott site became the gas company's Ordnance Wharf tar works. This included the Lennard still which had been developed by the firm. It produced naphtha and then creosote, used to preserve timber as well as carbolic acid and a residue, used for the manufacture of alizarine and finally, pitch used for making asphalt. In the 1970s the Lennard still which had stood disused for many years was restarted successfully as an experiment by staff at the Ordnance Tar Works, who later mounted an exhibition about it

The Lennard Still

BIPHOSPHATED GUANO

In the 1870s the Biphosphated Manure Co. also called the Biphosphated Guano Company was based at Ordnance Wharf. It seems to have been owned by Christopher Weguelin, a banker and Trustee of Morden College and a waiver was issued by the College in this instance. It was maybe thought that if such a works was tucked away at the tip of the Peninsula that the smells would not be noticed too much – but an accumulation of bad smells led to an enquiry and an investigation by the authorities in 1871.

The manufacture of 'artificial' manure was an important industry on Thameside in the 19th century. There were other such works on Greenwich Marsh. In Deptford a most important breakthrough had been made with the development of superphosphates by John Bennett Lawes, and Frank Hills used a similar process at his works in Riverway. All of these processes used up waste materials from other industries, a useful task but one which meant that a lot of smelly items were stored in the area.

Guano works however used compacted bird droppings. Biphosphated advertised their use of *'Finest Peruvian guano'* said to be *'a safer fertiliser to use than raw guano'*. They also sold 'Bolivian guano'.

Their works was taken over and closed by South Metropolitan Gas before their works was built. The guano companies had made protest about bad smells from the new gas works before it was built but this had been taken rather less seriously by the House of Lord than complaints from the Stockwell and Lewis ship yard.

MOCKFORDS ORDANCE MANURE WORKS

Mockford's 'Ordnance' Manure Works moved to Ordnance Wharf in 1873. They had come from the City of London, via Deptford, where they had been in the 'artificial manure' trade since at least the 1860s. They used South American guano, and 'shoddy', waste from fabric manufacture, along with sulphate of ammonia.

Ballard, the Government inspector found *'about 250 tons of shoddy on the premises, a considerable quantity of mineral phosphates, and over-5,000 tons of guano'*. They were producing sulphate of ammonia and 'probably' sulphuric acid, for the manure trade.

The process of manufacture led to 'corrosive vapours' and Ballard said 'the stench when these mixings are going on is simply intolerable'.

BRIQUETTES – WYLAM STEAM FUEL CO

Britquettes are cheap fuel made from mixtures of broken coal and dust pressed together with tar. It was a way of using up gas works waste tar and coal dust from anyone who had any. One such on the Greenwich Peninsula was the Wylam Steam (or Patent) Fuel Co. Although it might be assumed that the name 'Wylam' related to the coal mining district in the North East of England, in fact it seems to be the name of the factory owner - William Wylam - who had taken out three patents in the early 1840s for machinery with which to make artificial fuel.

Wylam's firm had previously been in Thames Street, Greenwich, and in 1847 obtained a lease from Morden College for a site on the Marsh. In 1846 local papers carried advertisements of more than a page of fine print extolling the virtues of Wylam's briquettes over all sorts of real coal, particularly Welsh coal, in every conceivable use. A year later they had their supplies of coal tar cut off by their suppliers, the Gas Light and Coke Co., for non payment of bills so they were probably not very prosperous. Despite this setback they were in a position to expand to a larger site in the mid-1860s and were the cause of complaint when they blocked the barge roads outside their wharf.

PERCIVAL PARSONS AND MANGANESE BRONZE

In the back streets of East Greenwich, barely on the Peninsula but just about on the edge of The River Gardens there is a short terrace of houses at right angles to Banning Street at the back of the Pelton Arms. This is the site of what was called The Thames Foundry, a working site so small it can only have been a local smithy. It was used by a Percival Parsons and we have to thank Neil Rhind for telling us about him.

Parsons worked hard on lots of inventions for the railways and for armament manufacture. In 1871 he supervised the building of the Bessemer works at East Greenwich and experimented at home on ways of boring guns. This led him to research various metals and alloys. Initially he produced a compound of zinc and lead which he called "white brass" which was used widely throughout the 19th century, especially in marine engines. After many more years work he produced a material with the strength of steel which would not corrode. This was manganese bronze - which he manufactured at the Thames Foundry.

In 1882, the Manganese Bronze and Brass Company opened to produce propellers in 'Parson's Manganese Bronze'. An adaption of this was their basic alloy for propeller production until about 1950. Stone's propeller works was not on the Peninsula, but just down the road in Charlton they made propellers for some very important and well known ships.

THOMAS ROBSON

So much of what we know about the past of local industry comes from newspaper reports of industrial accidents. Sometimes it is the only thing we know about a works and it also tells us something about the workforce and their background.

Thomas Robson had founded a firework factory in Greenwich in 1845. This fronted onto the Woolwich Road with an entrance roughly where the chip shop stands today. There was a path stretching back along the line of Glenforth Street to an area of land intersected by ditches and dykes. This is the now the site of Tunnel Avenue and the motorway. In this area were a number of huts in which work on the explosives was undertaken. Before the days of radio, fireworks were much more important in use as emergency and other signals.

Robson held patents for *'firing signals and other lights'*. The factory made a variety of signalling devices for ships and railways, fireworks for displays and other small devices, like 'caps'.

One item made there was a railway fog signal, which consisted of two small iron saucers, enclosing a small amount of gunpowder. 'Crimping' the cups together was done by hand, using screw presses, an operation which carried 'some risk'. In fact there was at least one accidental explosion a month but owing to a *'misunderstanding'*, Mr. Dyer had not reported these accidents to the Explosives Inspectorate. There was an iron shield, which moved between the worker and the explosives at the moment at which the pressing movement took place. Employees had to wear special shoes and fireproof clothes with no pockets in them.

20th November 1882 was Mary Mahoney's first day at work on the presses. There was a space of six feet by five for the two women to sit with about 800 explosive signals. Unknown to her supervisor Emily, Mary was putting the cups into the press in the wrong way. The foreman, Mr. Law, was outside the shed when he was knocked over by a series of explosions. He forced his way through the smoke to Mary who was on the floor with molten lead falling on her. He managed to get her out and she said '*Oh, Mr.Law*' as he tried to pull off her burning dress – and then he collapsed.

Mary was taken just across the road to the Workhouse Infirmary and died four days later 'of exhaustion'. She was twenty-four years old, and lived in Marsh Lane with her parents who had come from Kerry to work as labourers. They had a lodger Catherine Allman, who also worked at Dyer and Robson's. She also came from this overcrowded immigrant community.

On 11th June 1887 Catherine was at work making candles to be used as signals on the South Western Railway Steamers from Southampton. The explosion, when it came, was 'like the firing of a pistol'. It was a very hot day and it was thought some of the ingredients might have become unstable when warmed. Catherine was badly burnt but lived. Two others with her, Anne Lake and Mary Masters, died.

By chance, the Chief Inspector of Explosives, Vivien Majendie, lived in Victoria Way, well within earshot.

After 1900 The Blenheim Engineering Company took over part of the Robson site. They had originally been the Henry Rifled Barrel Engineering and Small Arms Co. It is possible, but unlikely, that actual rifles were made there. An accident there in 1902 was in the 'drying house for coloured stars' which sounds more like fireworks than actual guns,

There were a number of other cartridge and small-scale explosive factories in the area from the 1870s. One of these was the Gladstone Cartridge Co. which shared the site with Henry Bessemer. There was a *'terrible explosion'* there in 1872 with over 30 teenage girls injured and *"rolling in the mud to put out the flames"*. They were breaking up cartridges and it was reported no one knew what had caused the explosion.

HOUSES

As industry grew around the peninsula houses were needed for workers to live in. Housing around the tide mill and chemical works had begun as Ceylon Place but more terraces had been added by Frank Hills. Coles Child and Morden College had provided an estate of houses for workers on the coal wharves. Other housing soon grew up around East Greenwich, some of it private and speculative and some of it charitable. There was, for instance, a very considerable estate built by the Hatcliffe Charity.

Most of the housing in East Greenwich remains today but housing built on the Peninsula was swept away by the London County Council in the 1960s as slum clearance. This housing was partly speculative but mostly it was small terraces of cottages built by individual factories for their workers with larger houses for supervisory staff. There was a 'big' house at Enderby Wharf – Enderby House which remains - but there was also East Lodge on the east bank about which there is a substantial degree of mystery.

Charles Booth surveyed the area in 1899. His class-based colour coding for most of the Peninsula is light blue - which he classified as *'poor... a moderate family'* and found no areas which were *'vicious and semi criminal'*. He finds a scatter of houses marked as red for *'middle class'*, which would have been publicans and foremen. He noted one London County Council estate, Idenden Cottages, which he said look *'comfortable'*. Elsewhere housing was built for the workers at individual factories and he notes the inhabitants *'except for managers and publicans are all working men'*.

The earliest workplace housing, after Ceylon Place, appears to be four houses on the River bank by Enderby Wharf. By the 1850s there were more cottages connected to various cement works and built on Morden College land. Bethell's Cottages was built near Blackwall Point and over the next 20 years a number of other small estates were laid out. In 1866 a small and innovative estate was started by the Blakely Ordnance Company with four storey buildings for workers and cottages for the foremen, but this estate was never finished until taken over by the gas company nearly 20 years later. Barbara Ludlow noted in her analysis of the population of the Marsh in the 19th century that a high proportion of the incomers were Irish, come to work in the new factories. Houses built near the Ransome stone factory are shown in the census to have many occupants originating from the Ipswich area, who had presumably come with Ransome from his family's works there.

Perhaps the most exotic and unlikely housing on the Peninsula is the flat above the Blackwall Tunnel based in the entrance lodge. This was built to house the superintendant and the caretaker of the Tunnel - there was originally also a north gatehouse, which also including accommodation. They had two bedrooms, a living-room, scullery, larder and w.c. on the floor above the archway. A third bedroom and a cistern room occupied part of the roof space above. It is thought not to be in use as housing now.

This was not an area where middle class people came and it was not an area growing from an existing village or settlement. It was isolated housing built for incoming workers, many of whom, no doubt, had no intention of settling for long. By the 1860s there were shops as well as pubs but schools, churches and community buildings were in short supply.

EAST LODGE

A house appears to have been built, perhaps at the same time as the mill, and later called East Lodge. It stood at the end of what was once called Marsh Lane and later called Riverway. Today its site is under the flats which lie between the Pilot and the River. There is an element of mystery about this house.

There are several unsubstantiated stories of an earlier structure under East Lodge, of vaulted cellars and of a passageway which led out towards the road. In 1932 Anne Davies, who lived there as a girl recalled, in the Kentish Mercury, vaulted cellars 'like those at the College'. A number of ex-residents of Riverway recall cellars and passages. Mr. Bridgeman who was brought up in a coffee shop at the end of the terrace remembered an underground passage which ran to where East Lodge once stood.

East Lodge was probably built as part of the estate of George Russell which included a large tide mill slightly up river of the house and the cottages which we now see alongside the Pilot pub, which was also part of the estate. A house is mentioned in documents on George Russell's estate and legacies.

What has resisted explanation is a newspaper report from 1796 which describes a robbery 'at Mr. Russell's house …. which was entered by 12 men who bound everyone in the house with cords and carried off furniture, wearing apparel and plate' … they then went into a boat 'and put off for the other shore'. In the 1820s Russell's widow is described as having once lived at 'Mill Place, East Greenwich. Now there is no trace on any other part of the Greenwich Riverside of a house owned by a Mr. Russell and it is a mystery to where this could have been except his land on the site where the tide mill was later built. No house is shown here on earlier maps. So, where was it?

A house which appears to have been built in 1802 was part of the Chancery assessment of Russell's estate in 1802. But this lists two houses. One is The Mill House, where William Johnson, the mill designer, was living, and another where Thomas Taylor, the foreman, lived. Possibly one of these houses was The Pilot, the pub. A few years later when repair work was being done John Hall's foreman was living in 'the big house' on site.

Anne Davies, in her interview to the local paper, said the house had been built by a Mr. Hewes who was apparently 'rather a reprobate'. She described how, on Sunday evenings, he sat on a window sill of the upstairs ballroom, dangling his legs outside and blowing a horn to disturb the service held in the Thames Church Mission. It appears that in 1845 the house was let to a Jamet Thomas Hewes.

East Lodge
(Picture thanks to Maj Wastaffe)

Jamet Hewes was the son of a distinguished millwright and civil engineer, Thomas Cheek Hewes. He was supposed to have trained as a doctor in Edinburgh but somehow did not qualify. He had however sufficient means inherited from his father who died when he was in his early 20s. The money was however to be administered by trustees.

He eventually moved to East Lodge in the early 1840s. He was by this time Commodore of the Arundel Yacht Club and donating pieces of silver plate for the winners of races between Greenwich, Gravesend, Erith and elsewhere. He had his own yacht and also a 'cutter'. In 1845 he oversaw a change of name to the 'London Yacht Club' and East Lodge is described both as 'the *residence of the Commodore*' and '*Club House*'. It may be from this time that some of the fancy decorations at East Lodge originate, noted by Ann Davies and her sisters. *'the hall was paved with large squares of black and white marble and its ceiling was painted by Sir James Thornhill ..... after the style of the Painted Hall'*. Discounting Thornhill who died in 1734, there was still a ballroom, upstairs.

Yachting at this level is not cheap occupation however Jamet was also working at this time as a Professor of Animal Magnetism *'to insure relief to those deemed incurable'*. Jamet seems to have had a number of liaisons during this time, with young women to whom he may or may not have been married *(she said that the clergyman read something out of a book but she couldn't recall what it was)*. There were some accusations of forgery about the registration of the birth of a child, for which someone else went to jail. There were other children ('he had entertained the foolish idea of substituting a boy child instead of the girl'). He had also been 'an enormous drinker in his time'.

Jamet shot himself at the age of 73. He was by then living in Camberwell with a Henrietta Pimm. His death was followed by a court case on inheritance of his father's fortune by one of his possible children.

In the late 1870s the East Lodge became company housing for Frank Hills' works manager, Thomas Davies. His three daughters wrote and circulated a family newsletter about their lives, the family and their holidays. They remembered Christmas parties, walks down the lane, and honey for tea, meadows with buttercups, larks and pink and white hawthorn. They loved the garden overlooking the River, the shrubbery, the swing, and the summer house. They never mentioned the adjacent chemical works, or Cory's Atlas coal transhipment hulk out in the River. As serious young women they also organised improving lectures and concerts above the local shop.

The house was demolished at the start of the 20th century, and the site was part of the Redpath Brown structural steel works. When they closed down Greenwich Yacht Club moved into their old canteen, unaware of a previous club house which was once nearby.

New Millennium Experience closed Riverway and cut it off from the River. Now it is very difficult to work out where East Lodge one stood as new flats and shops have been built irrespective of the old site boundaries

Dick Norton and Fred at Norton's barge yard. Sheds on the foreshore here housed Greenwich Yacht Club.
(Photo thanks to Pat O'Driscoll)

PUBS

As well as having somewhere to live and somewhere to work, people need places for relaxation. The Greenwich peninsula may not have had anything much in the way of facilities up to around 1900 - but it did have some pubs. Some of them are still there.

CUTTY SARK TAVERN

Ballast Quay has had a complicated history of pubs over many years. Even more complex was Anchor Iron Wharf which is adjacent Ballast Quay but not really on Greenwich Marsh. A community has existing here since at least the late Saxon period and it can be assumed there has always been the establishment here of a predecessor public house.

The current pub is, of course, The Cutty Sark. It dates from around 1809 replacing a pub called The Green Man. It was originally called The Union Tavern – this being Union Wharf, as you can see from a newly painted street sign. It was renamed Cutty Sark in 1952 when the sailing ship was installed in a dry dock slightly up river. At some point in the early 1970s it was changed from a one bar local into its present layout with, I was told, 'a staircase built for Errol Flynn'.

Owned by Morden College since they built it in the early 19th century, it is now 'a Young's pub'.

SALUTATION TAVERN

On old maps there is a building which may have been a pub – and if so it is the most mysterious in the area. This was Salutation House, after which a modern street in the area was named. As a pub it could have been built to serve thirsty workers at the gunpowder works and later rope walk at Enderby Wharf – since there was nothing like enough housing there to support a pub. Or perhaps it was not a pub at all! It appears briefly in the early 19th century and then disappears and it is only a guess that it was a pub at all. There was already a 'Salutation House' in Church Street, Greenwich and another in Woolwich. 'Salutation House' was a common name for a public house at the time. This building however was isolated, inland with no obvious road or footpath access. A building is shown marked on a Morden College Survey plan of c. 1800 and can be seen on the 1843 tithe map and again in a Morden College deed of 1858 and on the 1880s Ordnance Map. The Morden College deed actually marks it as 'Salution' house so maybe it was not a pub but a 'Solution House' in use by the nearby the bleach works.

THE PILOT

The oldest pub actually on the Peninsula is clearly The Pilot dating from around 1802 and serving the local community in all that time as it was buiolt to do. It has changed a lot recently, from the little one bar local that many of us remember. It has now been taken over by a fashionable brewery, Fullers, and has a garden and an extension and a more than one room in which you can sit and drink. All of which would have been a bit of a shock to its previous clientele. Its history and naming are described in an earlier chapter.

The Pilot 1980s

THE SEA WITCH

The Sea Witch pub

As industry spread along the riverside so more public houses were opened by landowners and head leaseholders. On the riverbank Charles Holcombe built a public house called the Sea Witch. The site of the pub was later covered by Amylum's riverside laboratory block building that seemed to look very much like its predecessor. Today it awaits development. It was built by Charles Holcombe's builder, William Drew around 1846. It appears to have been originally called 'The Morden Castle' which was an 'Ale and Stout House'. In November 1849, it was put up for sale at auction.

The pub was, shortly afterwards, renamed 'The Sea Witch'. In a photograph of the 1930s the brewery is shown as a Whitbread house, but earlier it had been owned by Gurney Hanbury of Camberwell. The pub had a riverside garden separated from it by the roadway. 'Sea Witch' was probably named after a ship. It was a common ship name but the pub might have been named after the

American tea clipper of revolutionary design - which was soon to visit the Thames and held several sailing records at the time.

Another Sea Witch was a British vessel, built in Blackwall Yard, just across the River from the pub, at around the same time. Both were built as 'opium clippers' - that is, built to take opium to China and return with tea, silk and other commodities. The pub was destroyed in 1940 by bombing but was in any case in a very dilapidated and rundown state.

STAR IN THE EAST

Alongside the Blackwall Tunnel entrance is a building which was the Star in the East Pub. When built it would have been outside the Bessemer Works and in the neighbourhood of many other factories. This building is now used by the electrical dealer, Ranworth, next to the northbound Blackwall Tunnel entrance. The pub was certainly there in 1865 when it was advertised for sale as a 'Public House and Spirit Stores'.

In 1898 the landlord was fined when the court heard a number of conflicting stories concerning an Ellen Pope who had drunk too much gin and bitters. The magistrate had accepted the police version that the landlord had served a drunken person.

Like Sea Witch the name may relate to a ship. Another ship was built at Blackwall Yard soon after Sea Witch, and also used for the opium trade in 1850. She was called Star in the East

ORDNANCE ARMS - MECHANICS' ARMS - KENILWORTH CASTLE

Another pub was Ordnance Arms in Blackwall Lane – no doubt named for the Blakeley Ordnance Works which was briefly built nearby in the mid-1860s. The pub was advertised as a 'wine and spirit establishment'. In the 1890s an inquest was held there on a baby, Hannah Whitehouse, who drowned in a nearby ditch while her brother and sister were chasing ducks – a vivid reminder of the marshy, semi-rural nature of the area despite all the industry.

The Mechanic's Arms' was built in 1869 on the north side of Morden Wharf Road. The first licensee in 1870 was William Drew who was also land owner Charles Holcombe's builder. The pub was demolished in the late 1890s as part of the Blackwall Tunnel construction.

Nearby was another pub, this one called the Kenilworth Castle in Ordnance Crescent. It was demolished when the Blackwall Tunnel was built. Unlike the others its name does not refer to a clientele from a local factory and very little is known about it.

THE MITRE

The Mitre Pub was built in the 1880s on Blackwall Lane to provide for thirsty gas workers. The South Metropolitan Gas Company granted a lease to the Courage Brewery. This is surprising, since the Company held a very strong line on temperance and the Chairman, George Livesey, was a national figure in the 'Band of Hope' In the 1960s it became a venue for local bands - in particular the very wonderful Wally Butcher and the Laughing Gravy Orchestra. International jazz star Dudu Pukwana played to a miniscule audience on Sunday lunch times.

Eventually the pub became home to Malcolm Hardee's notorious Tunnel Club (Alternative Comedians v. The Eltham Boys). Once all the acts had been booed off, Malcolm would usually do anything – and I mean anything - on stage that the audience asked. It later became a night club with constant name changes and a bad reputation. A terrace was built outside, advertising itself as 'just like Ibiza'. There were murders and arrests. A visit inside revealed a decor of pink, black and gold quilted plastic.

In 2016 it was burnt down, with one staff death. Fourteen people were arrested for arson and then released. It has been rebuilt in a different style to the pub and appears to have reopened following a row with the local Planning Department. It is now Studio 338, or – has been changed yet again.

The Mitre in the 1980s

GREENWICH TOWN SOCIAL CLUB

Slightly down Blackwall Lane from the Ship and Billet is Greenwich Town Social Club – recently rebuilt and not yet reopened as I write this. Despite being a member I do not know when it opened. It appears at 10 Blackwall Lane in a local directory of 1919.

The building recently demolished was clearly post Second World War and the original building may have been destroyed in bombing, there was a V1 hit nearby. It is Clubs and Institutes' Union registered and run by a committee of local people.

MEANTIME

What the Peninsula does have – in its non-regenerated area - is a new brewery, Meantime. This was founded in 1999 by Alastair Hook who trained at the brewing school of the Technical University of Munich. He started the brewery in a small lock-up on an industrial estate in Charlton before moving to the site on Blackwall Lane in 2010 and by 2013 they were producing 50,000 hectolitres with a growth rate of 60% per year. They were brewing a range of twelve beers which focused on traditional British and European styles such as Lager, Pale Ale, Porter and India Pale Ale. In addition, there are a range of limited edition seasonal ales. They now have a visitor centre in Blackwall Lane as well as the Tasting Rooms bar and a Brewery Shop.

In 2015 the brewery was sold to major international brewer SAB Miller and later to Asahi Group Holdings of Japan. Meantime has become a major brewer, but its sale to an international brewery, owed by the Japanese, could mean the end of brewing in Greenwich and a move to the Fullers brewery in Chiswick, owned by the same company.

Regeneration post-2000 has brought many more licensed premises to the Peninsula. Clearly there are many in the Dome – they are not serving a local clientele and can be ignored! Outside of the Dome there are bars like Greenwich Kitchen which are neither pub nor restaurant,

And Enderby House is likely to be opened as a pub by Young's.

DOCKS, THE RIVER AND RAILWAYS

Up until the middle of the 19th century the main transport link between East Greenwich industries and the rest of the world was the River. Transport infrastructure therefore is not just about roads and railways. Managing ships on the overcrowded River in the 19th century was an issue of great concern and something which needed to be dealt with by an official body.

The Harbour Master's house sits at the end of Ballast Quay on the corner with Pelton Road. It is a big house and prominent but very few people will have any idea what it was for and who the Harbour Master was.

The River is an empty place now but until the 1970s it was busy with ships from all over the world. We think of the days of sail bringing 'the spices of the east' into London but the majority of ships coming up London River brought coal from Durham and Northumberland to power London's industry. In the 17th century 200 collier ships supplied London and by the end of the 18th century about a million tons of 'sea coal' a year was coming in. Collier ships created an unregulated chaos in the River.

In order to try and sort this out Harbour Masters were appointed for stretches of River between Gravesend and the Tower and their job was to allow vessels to proceed up stream in rotation. They were appointed under the Port Act of 1799 and subsequent by-laws determined specified moorings where not more than 15 ships at a time could wait. Flags were raised to tell vessels to proceed to a wharf for unloading or to remain where they were. The original Greenwich Harbour Masters Office was in Highbridge Place, probably adjacent to the Drawdock which is still at the end of Eastney Street.

In the 1850s the current Harbour Master's House on Ballast Quay was built, designed by George Smith. It closed, along with the system of regulation, in the 1890s and has been a private house ever since.

These days the tiny numbers of vessels which come up the River are regulated through Barrier Control, the Navigation Centre, run by the Port of London Authority at the Thames Barrier.

THE ANGERSTEIN RAILWAY

The Peninsula has its own railway running down its eastern boundary. At one time a branch went all the way down to the Dome. So what is this railway and when and why was it built?

Angerstein is a name which keeps cropping up in the East Greenwich area. It originates with the romantic figure of John Julius Angerstein - a Russian financier with mysterious, possibly illustrious, origins. He may well have been the son of the Empress Ann of Russia and a British banker. He spent a long working life in the City of London, regularised Lloyds of London, and his art collection provided the foundation of the National Gallery. Angerstein, is one of a number of influential people who can be said to have shaped the Marsh and its industries. His country home was built to overlook the area of the Marsh itself, and is now Woodlands, used by the Steiner School, in Mycenae Road.

Angerstein and his family, went on to acquire, by 1856, a large stretch of land on the east side of the Peninsula between the River and the Dover Road. In 1850 Julius's son John must have seen the stretch of land between Blackheath and the River as full of potential. The North Kent railway line was being built through a tunnel which ran from Blackheath to a point adjacent to his land. All that would be needed was a wharf and a connecting railway and good business would be guaranteed.

A railway was planned in 1851 to run on Angerstein's land from the North Kent Railway to a riverside wharf. Built on private land there was no need for an Act of Parliament except for the bridge needed to cross Woolwich Road, then the Lower Turnpike

Road between Greenwich and Woolwich. The Act was applied for and passed in May 1851.

The line opened in 1852 but had already been leased to the South Eastern Railway for operation. The spoil removed from the Blackheath/Charlton railway tunnel was used to build the embankment on which the railway goes on its way to the River. It runs parallel with Lombard's Wall, the Tudor flood defence and property marker.

The railway line was, and has remained, entirely a goods line. As industry grew in East Greenwich and Charlton so it grew and was extended. In the 1890s the line was extended right across the Peninsula to enter the gas works via a bridge across Riverway.

In 2018 Angerstein Wharf handles aggregate which is carried along the old railway line and which it is soon to be upgraded.

THE DOCK THAT NEVER WAS

In the mid 19th century the Peninsula was seen as a useful site for a dock.

In the 1850s dock construction was booming in London. In the late 1850s plans were made which would have entirely changed the face of the Greenwich Peninsula. The plans were repeated in the 1880s but there is just the suspicion of hype about them.

Railways were being planned all round the country. The Mercers' Company recorded approaches in this period from several railway companies who wanted to build over, or near, their land on the Peninsula. In December 1852 they, like Morden College, were approached by the South Eastern Railway, in connection with an extension of the Angerstein line and a plan to join it both to Blackwall via a ferry and the Greenwich Railway from London Bridge. This appears to have come to nothing.

In May 1853 the Mercers' were approached by the, otherwise unknown, Charlton and Blackwall Railway. It was hinted that docks were actually what they were planning. Then, in 1857 there was a sudden new departure. An application was made to Parliament for a large dock to be built on the Greenwich Peninsula.

In this period Greenwich saw a large number of Parliamentary elections and by-elections with some lively campaigns – at a time when two members were elected to Parliament by Greenwich voters. They included local industrialists, like Peter Rolt, colourful local characters like John Townsend, and David Salomans the first Jewish Member of Parliament. Another contestant was William Angerstein. Local people and local industrialists threw themselves into these elections and one of the most assiduous was Coles Child. In this context it should be noted that Coles Child was a director of the South Eastern Railway during the 1850s.

It might be assumed that the South Eastern Railway was behind the great dock scheme in that it was to be renamed the 'Greenwich and South Eastern Docks.' Plans of the proposed dock show an enormous scheme which would have taken up most of the land on the Peninsula. The length of the dock was to run north-south down the length of the land. The whole structure was to be in a 'T' shape so that the main north-south dock was met by another at right angles with entrances at Enderby's Wharf to the west, and the end of what is now Riverway in the east - where it would also have met the Angerstein Railway.

The scheme was noted with approval by the *Kentish Mercury* in 1858 just before yet another election. Their leader writer spoke of the miserable time people were having in Greenwich 'the silence is only broken at intervals by the sepulchral sound of the wheels of an empty omnibus.... even if you see some active pedestrian approaching the public baths, from having nothing else do to, his gloomy countenance renders it doubtful whether he is about to enter for the purposes of ablution or to drown himself'.

In 1858 the Dock was being presented as part of a package. The North and South Metropolitan Junction Railway would change everything – making travel throughout the capital easy and bringing peace and prosperity to Greenwich. At the same time another election was under way and one of the candidates was William Angerstein who had inherited the land around the Angerstein Railway. A letter to the Mercury from '*A Reader*' said "At last there seems a chance of poor Greenwich being resuscitated and rising from the ashes. I and others have hailed the advent of the Greenwich and South Eastern Docks".

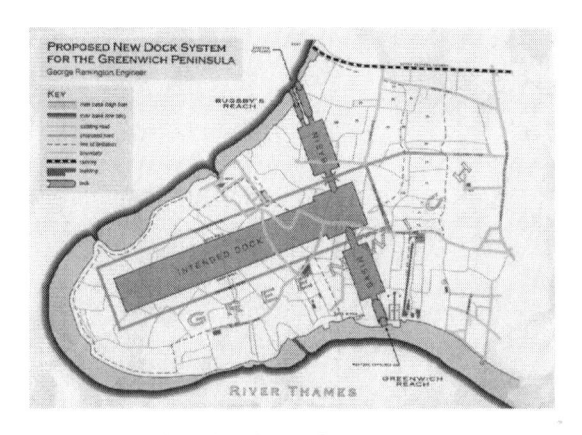

Drawing thanks to Chris Grabham

The question was, of course, where did the candidates for Parliament stand on this issue? Votes were not secret then and in the run up to any election the *Mercury* was happy to print on its front page lists of names of voters with their voting intentions, week by week, as the election approached.

On December 2nd '*Straight*' wrote to the *Mercury* and enquired whether the candidates would '*put their hands in their pockets ... and assist projects*'. The *Mercury's* leader writer was happy to point out that some 40 acres of land which would be needed to build the dock were owned by William Angerstein.

In the following weeks Mercury Coles Child asked if Angerstein would be prepared to '*make the Company a present of the land required*'? Needless to say this gift was not forthcoming from Angerstein who went on to lose the election.

A SECOND DOCK SCHEME

After 1859 the issue of the dock scheme went very quiet. It was raised again in the 1860s but nothing came of any of it. The dock scheme came up again in the 1880s. Ostensibly it was not put forward by the South Eastern Railway although, as they paid for the parliamentary deposit, it must have had something to do with them. It no longer included a dock along the length of the Peninsula, only the cross head of the 'T' junction. It proved a severe embarrassment to the South Metropolitan Gas Company whose East Greenwich works were then under consideration. Nothing came of that either.

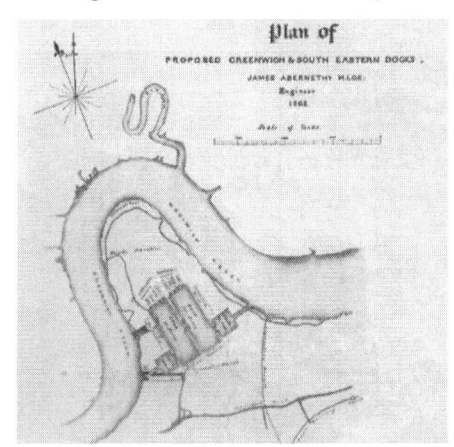

ROADS

What did not change on the Peninsula was the road layout, which had to wait until the 20th century and the Blackwall tunnel. There was a tram route on the Peninsula.

Trams were quite a big thing in Greenwich. On the edge of Peninsula alongside the Angerstein line and fronting on Woolwich Road was the Central Repair Depot, latterly known as the Airfix Building. Further down Woolwich Road in Charlton was the Tramatorium where old trams were broken up and burnt. Most important was Greenwich Power Station still with us and standing just up river of Ballast Quay.

Trams in the late 19th century were run by private companies. From 1881, the trams in the Woolwich area were horse drawn and operated by the Woolwich and South East London Tramways Company. One line from Woolwich finished at Old Woolwich Road, where it met the line of the London Tramways Company. They had a depot on the future power station site. In 1896, the London County Council Act gave the Council powers to operate its own tram services and they took over the London Tramways Company in 1899 and, later in 1905, the Woolwich and South East London Tramway Company. In 1903 LCC began to electrify the tramways.

The tramway from the Woolwich Road to the Blackwall Tunnel was new and built as part of the LCC's scheme to extend electric tramways into South East London. This line ran up Blackwall Lane and to the newly constructed Tunnel Avenue. It opened for passengers in 1906. Electrification of all these lines used the conduit system (i.e. power rails in a slot in the road surface), rather than overhead wires. The power for these trams eventually came from Greenwich Power station

A preserved tram telephone box stood in Blackwall Lane alongside Ranworth"s shop. Sadly it was swept away as part of a 'tidying up' operation for the 2014 Olympics.

THE BLACKWALL TUNNELS

The Blackwall 'Tunnel - when it was built it was described as the 'Twenty-first Wonder of the World'. Pall Mall Gazette said *'Londoners have been ignorant of the fact that they themselves were carrying out one of the greatest engineering feats in the history of the world ...... perhaps London will wake up and realise what it has accomplished.*

As the 19th century drew to a close so roads began to become more important – and so did a need to cross the River without recourse to a boat. Everybody nowadays hates the 'old' Blackwall Tunnel with its five bends and far too much heavy traffic. However the Tunnel was a major piece of infrastructure to come to Greenwich Marsh, an engineering achievement designed with a strong concept of public benefit. Something we should be proud of. Today it carries 50,000 motor vehicles a day but it was built for pedestrians and horses and carts

Up until 1894 there were no river crossings down river of the Tower apart from numerous ferries. Up-river bridges were all tolled, except for those owned by the City of London. As more bridges were built the cost of crossing the River became a matter of enormous concern. In 1877 the Metropolitan Toll Bridges Act was passed to allow the Metropolitan Board of Works to buy the bridges and make the free from tolls. the remarkable David Salomans then MP for Greenwich played a major part in the parliamentary process leading to this act and he was very aware that people down river of the Tower did not have these free crossings and that a programme should be set up to provide free crossing for east Londoners. Committees sat and various schemes were put forward.

In 1897 a new Act of Parliament enabled the Metropolitan Board of Works to provide a river crossing at Blackwall. An initial proposal was drawn up by Joseph Bazalgette but before work could start the Metropolitan Board of Works was abolished to be replaced by the London County Council. This was the first London wide body to be elected and at its first meeting on the

22nd of March, 1889, it agreed a contract for the new Tunnel at Blackwall. The foot tunnels and the Free Ferry followed

The Blackwall Tunnel was opened by the Prince of Wales in 1897 apparently following a banquet in the Tunnel. I remember being told that two nights later the Poplar Boys met the Greenwich Boys down in the Tunnel – just to sort a few things out.

It was designed by the LCC.s engineer Alexander Binnie and built by Pearsons who had just finished the Hudson River Tunnel in New York. We all need to realise how revolutionary it was both in concept and design. It was the longest tunnel which had ever been built under a river. Like other tunnels it was built with a tunnelling shield, a development of the design introduced by Marc Brunel for the Thames Tunnel at Rotherhithe in 1825–43. The shield used at Blackwall was built by Easton & Anderson of Erith and was a giant steel cylinder divided so as to allow as many as 12 men to be at the work-face. When it was ready it was finally lined with white-glazed tiles specially designed by T. & R. Boote of Burslem. The roadway was paved with granite setts.

During building there was a scheme for monitoring the health effects of the work on workers. Although it was built for pedestrians and horses drawn traffic its designers cannot have had the smallest concept of what it has to handle today. Horses were banned after the Second World War – and today a single pedestrian will cause the Tunnel to be shut and south east London traffic to come to a standstill.

In those days people could walk through the Tunnel and there were staircases for pedestrians. One of these is near Ordnance draw dock. The shafts themselves were enormous double-skinned cylinders of iron made by Thames Iron Works & Ship Building Company, just across the River at the mouth of the River Lea. They were and lined inside with glazed brickwork and at either end were fitted with spiral staircases for pedestrians, and domed over with glass-and-iron roofs. They were closed to pedestrians in the 1960s. Now used as ventilation shafts the domed roofs are now designed to 'open like the petals of a flower' to allow fumes to escape,

It was also possible to walk into the Tunnel from near the entrance. On the parallel section of Tunnel Avenue there is a cross over point and beside it one of the original pillars in polished red granite from which there would have been stone steps leading down to the roadway. This now stands at the end of a ramp from the Tunnel Approach road, built in the early 1990s so that over height lorries could be diverted before they entered the Tunnel. On the crossover point stood a concrete building. When the area began to be 'tidied up' for the opening of the Dome in 2000 it was thought to be ugly, but there was some question about what it was for. Why was it there?? It seemed to date from the Second World War and was thought to be a defence structure with equipment to shut off the Tunnel in an emergency. It was however removed as unfitting.

Our southern end of the Tunnel still has its original gatehouse – while that at the northern end was demolished when the 'new' tunnel was built in the mid-1960s. The gatehouse is in 'Arts and Crafts Scots-Baronial style' in red and yellow sandstone. On it is shown '1897' and 'Blackwall Tunnel' flanked by shields bearing the arms of Surrey and Kent and on the wall is a bronze dedication plaque by Singer & Son recording the opening of the Tunnel plus a bare-breasted female and the bearded head of a river god. There is also a relief of a section of the Tunnel with construction work in progress. The shame is that we all go through so fast that no one stops to look at these. I have already given some details of the flat inside the gatehouse.

The Tunnel was to be accessed by Tunnel Avenue, running down the Peninsula from a junction with the Woolwich Road. It was eventually flanked at that junction by East Greenwich Library, built in 1905 and the Fire Station built in 1902. It is instructive to learn that as early as 1934, Greenwich Labour Party felt it necessary to protest at the dangers of this junction. In 2020 work is yet again about to start in an attempt to make it safer. When built, Tunnel Avenue was grandly planted with plane trees as it progressed smoothly down to meet the new Tunnel. In the 1950s it also suffered from the likes of young Dave Carpenter, coming home on his Norton Excelsior, at ten at night, changing up a gear on every bend and coming out at 95, having disabled the silencer in Poplar.

In those days the Tunnel was, dangerously, two way - with the hazard, described by Dave Carpenter, of two lorries meeting on a bend, and both refusing to give way. Since then over-height lorries have become the problem with a specials system installed with a network of gantries, sensors, cameras and ultimately the police. If the vehicle has got as far as the slope into the Tunnel, and is stopped at the lights, the driver is treated to a telling-off over loudspeakers for all to hear before being removed up the escape ramp.

The original public transport service through the Tunnel was a Tilling horse bus starting in 1897. Since then there is the 108 bus. London's first single-deck motor bus route was route 69 through Blackwall Tunnel, introduced in 1912 and starting from Plumstead. The police would not then allow double deckers though the Tunnel. The bus was apparently running through the Tunnel from 1914 between Bow and Blackheath. By 1922 it was running between Clapton Ponds and Lee Green, and then on to Forest Hill. In 1924 it became the 108. double deckers were tried from 1927. The route was later spilt because of low bridges and the northern section became the 208. In 1937 two batches of double decker buses were specially built for use in the Blackwall with specially shaped roofs to improve clearance on the corners. The last solid-tyred AEC bus in London operated on route 108. The 108 has had many variations of its route over the years but keeps on running.

Motor transport grew and grew and the original tunnel was barely coping by the 1930s. The London County Council got an Act of Parliament in 1938 for a new tunnel but could not build it because of the Second World War. Work began in 1960 and the 'new' Tunnel was opened in 1967 by Desmond Plummer Tory Leader of the Greater London Council. This information is written in large enough letters for every Tunnel user to see as they enter the Tunnel – much larger than anything about the Prince of Wales and the 'old' Tunnel. The new Tunnel is wider and higher. It has no bends but it does have ventilation towers designed by Terry Farrell and they are listed.

We are now being threatened with a third tunnel which will turn sharply east from the Peninsula and go to Silvertown. The original approach road ran through an area which was not 'developed' although it was used for market gardens and some grazing. What we do not seem to have is an evaluation of how the tunnel of the 1890s and its approach road have influenced the development of the area over the past 130 years.

The Blackwall Tunnel was a great engineering achievement, and a moral one in providing a free crossing downriver of the Tower. It has allowed a vast increase in motorised cross river traffic. What would we have there if it had not been built?

THE 20TH CENTURY

THE KNACKERS

When the area was semi-rural there were many horses grazing in the fields who worked in the cab trade. As time went by many of the horses to be seen in the fields were actually waiting their turns for slaughter at the knackers, Harrison Barber, in Blackwall Lane. This was a site on the Peninsula which was most illustrative of 20th century changes.

The Greenwich depot of Harrison, Barber & Co was one of several owned by this firm which also seems to have had contracts with tramlines, local authorities and others using horses in transport. They were quoted on the stock exchange and described as oversubscribed and a premium company in the years before the Great War. They were sited more or less where Blackwall Lane is crossed by the Tunnel Approach – on the east side and thus slightly south of the Holiday Inn.

What replaced the horses was the internal combustion engine. Garages and motor repair depots were opening quickly. In 1933 the opening of Crossways Service Station was a sign of the times. This was next to the knackers – so the horses' last moments on earth before their execution would be the sight of their real killer - the motor car.

ELECTRICITY

With the new century came a new source of power. The new power station was built near the site of the tide mill at the end of Riverway on land which had been the western end of Frank Hills' chemical works. It became known as Blackwall Point Power Station – despite being a very long way from Point Wharf. It was built by the Blackheath and Greenwich Electric Light Co and it began to supply local people in 1900. It generated power using steam engines fuelled with coal delivered to a big new jetty. The Company's name was later changed to the South Metropolitan Electric Light and Power Company Ltd.

The East Greenwich tide mill had been almost the latest thing in 1803 - a machine to harness the power of the tidal river. It was overtaken by steam - power generated from coal and then the gas works. There was no concept then of giant power stations and there was no national grid. Early power stations provided electricity to quite small local areas and many were started by the local authorities. In Greenwich a private company undertook this role.

The new power station was called 'The Powerhouse' and it eventually had a capacity of 15,000 kW. It was designed by Reginald P. Wilson and much of the equipment came from Johnson and Phillips based just up the road in Victoria Way. The company's electrical engineer was John Archibald Constable, described as a pioneer of the electrical engineering industry.

Sited beside the River the subsoil on which it was built was not good and it appeared that soap works refuse had been dumped there, so the whole of the power station was built on piles made of pinewood. The buildings are described as substantial but the lack of money meant they were not "interesting from an architectural point of view" except that the engine room was said to be faced with white glazed bricks. There was also a large and prominent chimney the height of which was considered 'excessive' by a local commentator.

The first power station lasted nearly 40 years, and then in 1939 South Metropolitan Electricity Company decided to replace it. It was eventually closed and demolished in 1947. Nationalisation overtook them before it was finished and the new Blackwall Point power station opened in 1952. The new power station was bigger, although limited by its narrow site. For this reason the administration and amenity block was built on the south side of Riverway - connected by an overhead bridge.

> **THE SOUTH METROPOLITAN ELECTRIC LIGHT AND POWER COMPANY, LIMITED.**
>
> ALL COMMUNICATIONS TO BE ADDRESSED TO THE COMPANY AT THE REGISTERED OFFICES.
> TELEGRAMS: POWERHOUSE, LONDON
> ENGINEER'S DEPARTMENT
> GENERATION
> POWER HOUSE, EAST GREENWICH, S.E.
> DISTRIBUTION
> 183 & 185 HIGH STREET, LEWISHAM, S.E.
> REGISTERED OFFICES
> 183 & 185, High Street, Lewisham. Novr. 26th, 1908

A jetty was built for ships up to 3,000 tons and with facilities so that waste ash and dust could be loaded into barges. It is this jetty which is now used for a gardening and community project. Three mills ground the coal into dust before it was fed to each boiler. Three turbo-generators worked to provide the power. In 1953 it was rated the eleventh most efficient power station in the country.

Six months after it closed in June 1980 a group from the Greater London Industrial Archaeology Society visited the site. They were able to actually enter one of the boilers and spend time in the coal handling plant. From the roof they noted *'a magnificent view of the surrounding industrial landscape'* – who would have believed that soon all this would have gone and that the site on which they stood would remain derelict for the next twenty years.

Up until the 1970s the Peninsula was a busy industrial area and the 20th century was to see a number of large works along with increasing amounts of warehousing as wharves changed hands

LINOLEUM

Linoleum was the universal floor covering of the Victorians, although it later enjoying a rather down-market image. Oil based floor coverings had evolved during the course of the 19th century and many linoleum factories had replaced 'floor cloth factories' like the Greenwich 'kampultican' factory. Linoleum manufacture was, however, down to one man, Frederick Walton.

Walton was the son of an inventor and an inventor he grew up to be. He set himself to find a use for something usually wasted, oxidised oil – the skin on the top of paint. The material he developed could be rolled out onto a suitable backing, using linseed oil and cork. Linoleum was the final product. Walton's first factory was in Chiswick in 1861, and he later moved to a bigger works at Staines.

The Staines works became very large and successful but Walton was to go off and leave it. He seems to have quarrelled with his managers over new developments and determined to go somewhere else with another new invention. That somewhere else was Greenwich. Walton had developed linoleum because he was interested in the raw materials it used, now he sought to mechanise the process.

A lease was taken out on part of Victoria Wharf and he installed three enormous machines there. By 1910 the works had become immense and he eventually took on another site slightly further north on part of Bethell's Wharf. Here they made about 20 miles of linoleum each week – a year's output would have stretched to Warsaw! They used a mixture of cork, oils and colouring. Each sheet was made of tens of thousands of tiny pieces – made up in an original pattern into a template by specialist craftsmen. A vast machine – 50 feet high and weighing 400 tons – produced huge sheets of lino in six different colours. These sheets were then cut and welded into the different designs.

Walton himself died in his nineties in 1921 following a car accident at Nice in the South of France. In his later years he had spent much of his time in pursuit of psychic phenomena. The Greenwich Inlaid Lino works had been closed during the Great War and reopened in the 1920s. However the company finances had became very insecure. The company was taken over by Michael Nairn of Kirkaldy in 1922, following a number of angry meetings, Nairn's kept the factory working through the 1920s and in 1926 the Duke of York, the future George VI, visited. The factory was then very prosperous and he toured it, wearing overalls. Greenwich Linoleum was made in the standard geometrical patterns fashionable at the time. Some specialist lino was also made - some for Lyons teashops with the Lyons name specially printed on it.

The Greenwich factory closed after the Second World War. At Kirkaldy in Nairn's archives are catalogues for Greenwich Linoleum which date from the 1940s - but they may be using a brand name after the factory in Greenwich had closed. One of the giant Greenwich machines was taken to Kirkcaldy but it is now long gone although lino is still made in the town.

Forbo Nairn, Michael Nairn's successor company, is now part of a Swiss based multinational. Nairn's sell varieties of linoleum again, but they call it 'Marmoleum'. They stress the natural products used - linseed and hessian - and the traditional designs. Linoleum is, they say, an environmentally friendly product - clean and natural - an interesting contrast to its high-tech sales pitch a hundred years ago.

VICTORIA DEEP WATER TERMINAL

The site of the lino factory on Victoria Wharf was eventually to become the current Hanson concrete batching factory. The linoleum factory was replaced by the Metropolitan Storage and

Trade Co. Ltd and in 1970 by the Victoria Deep Water Terminal. This was a specialist wharf for handling containers. In 1987 40,000 boxes were being handled on the wharf every year – well below its actual capacity. The two gantry cranes, painted in brilliant colours, were a landmark on the River and hated by incoming yuppies on the Isle of Dogs.

Since 1990, the site has received aggregates under a succession of operators. The terminal now handles vessels of up to 8000 tonnes. It is now used by Hanson as an aggregate and concrete batching plant. Circular sections for tunnels are made here.

REDPATH BROWN – STRUCTURAL STEEL

Redpath Brown was an Edinburgh based company dealing with structural steel. In 1903 they opened a London branch and moved to a hitherto unused site south of Riverway. Spoil from the Blackwall Tunnel had been dumped there and much work was needed to make the ground acceptable for a large works. They were in the area between Riverway and the Pilot and John Harrison Way which is now largely flats.

In 1929 the Company merged with Dorman Long and later a site known as 'Dorman Long' was added to the Greenwich works. This seems to have operated only as a depot and to have been a completely separate establishment.

Redpath Brown provided the structural steel for many important buildings in London from the Greenwich works. This almost certainly included the Festival Hall, several power stations and other major buildings. A local example is the railway bridge just outside Lewisham station built as an emergency after the St.John's railway disaster of 1956 and still in place. They also undertook an important role in the Second World War in the construction of landing craft. The works was nationalised with the rest of the steel industry and was known as 'Riverside Steel Works'.

They closed in the 1980s and the site was taken over as a police riot training ground – to some consternation from locals, and the Council, who had not been informed. Later many of the buildings were converted for use as a trading estate and the canteen became the base for Greenwich Yacht Club. All of this was pulled down for the Millennium Celebrations as being untidy.

Redpath Brown had a large jetty which lay between the end of Riverway and the current Yacht Club. It was occupied by a different and separate yacht club run by Kenny. The jetty had a Derek Jarman style garden. He used to advertise on the Blackwall Tunnel Approach 'drinks and music by the riverside' – i.e. sitting on an old box with a can of beer and Kenny's radio. It was actually very pleasant but New Millennium Experience did not think it looked quite tidy enough and following a long press campaign Kenny was forced to leave.

DELTA METAL – BRONZE

The largest and best known metal producer on the Peninsula was the Delta Metal Company. Delta was, and is, a very important company which was still in business at their Greenwich site well into the 1980s, specialising in a range of bronzes. The site is now used as the golf range

Alexander Dick had come to England from Europe in the 1880s. He was of British descent, but born and educated in Germany and had worked in Spain and France. In England he established the Phosphor Bronze Company in New Cross and managed it until 1882. In 1883 he began to work on brass and other alloys and, in particular, added iron to brass. The resulting alloy was named 'Delta Metal' and this name was the registered trademark.

Dick also adapted an extrusion process for the production of brass rod. This process was first used at New Cross in the early 1890s and in 1905 the Greenwich site was opened as the Extruded Metals Company Ltd. During the next seventy years the works grew to take over much of the area along the north eastern riverfront as other works closed down.

The Great War brought Delta increased business and also competition. The Dick family continued to manage the company throughout consolidation up to 1940. In the Second World War metal manufactured at East Greenwich found its way into other works up and down the country.

Delta boasted that 'by the end of the war there was hardly even a repair garage of any size in the land which did not have lathes, drilling and milling machines installed and working day and night turning out metal parts for war uses...the parts were produced from Delta extruded bars'. Their products were used in 'fuses and primers for shells, for parts and fittings of guns and torpedoes, for searchlights, and Radar apparatus, and all the other innumerable scientific instruments, telephone parts, aircraft fittings, ship construction angles, tee and channel bars, and other sections for ships' fittings.. used in craft of all kinds from the largest battleships to the smallest launches; components of vehicles from tanks to lorries, of speedometers, lighting equipment and "Mulberry," "Pluto" and "Fido".

Delta Dispatch Dept.

They had a 500 ft long jetty with 16 feet depth of water at high water. After the Second World War Delta were to use much of their huge site for warehousing but the company itself moved on from strength to strength, to become a successful multi-national. Experimental work on bronzes continued at Greenwich throughout the 1960s and 1970s but this works, where their large-scale manufacture started, was closed apparently unnoticed in the 1980s. Some work was undertaken in Greenwich on the old Johnson and Phillips site in Charlton, but in the 1990s Delta left Greenwich altogether.

MOLASSINE

In the twentieth century the Greenwich waterfront became known as a place of very bad smells. In a history of the Molassine works written in the 1950s the company said how everyone who went past on the River knew them from the dramatic sight of their large molasses tanks – local people were more likely to know them by the dramatic smells which came from the works!

Molassine made animal foodstuffs and is still a trade name for cattle feed sold to farmers. Locally they will be best remembered for Vims dog biscuits. These were based on molasses and the firm was founded in 1900 to exploit this. The recipe came from an eastern European called Arthur Stein who vanished in Prague during the Second World War. Molassine moved to Greenwich around 1908 buying molasses from Tate & Sons at refinery at Silvertown. They built the steel tanks to hold the molasses between 1910 and 1914.

One of their main products was feed for horses, made from sphagnum moss mixed with molasses made from both sugar beet and sugar cane. As well as Vims they made another dog food, Stims. The yard sweepings from these products were mixed with rough pieces of sphagnum moss and sold as Rito, a garden fertiliser.

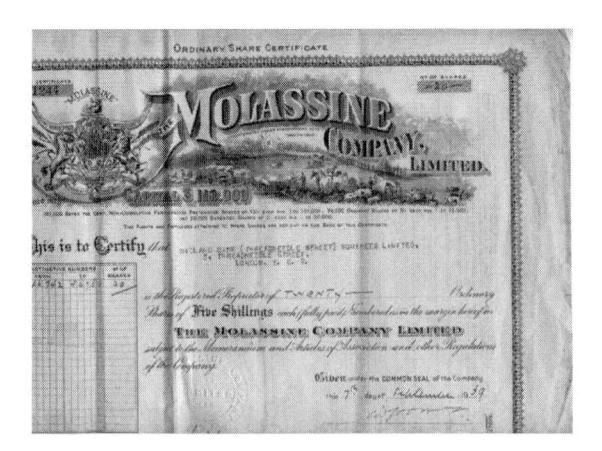

I have been shown a tin Matchbox with the Molassine Trade mark on the front – while on the reverse side was a 'reclining naked lady holding a tray or plate with one elbow resting on a Pig'.

During the Great War their feed mix was used by soldiers as an antiseptic plaster for wounds. In the 1950s and 1960s they used comedian Norman Wisdom whose films almost always included references to Vims, sometimes as part of the plot. Another artist was Petula Clark – then known as 'little Pet Clark' featuring in their pet food advertisements.

The animal feed business in Greenwich was closed in 1981and machinery was transferred to Rumenco at Burton on Trent, who continue to use the trade name.

What remains is their jetty – now called Primrose Pier and the large red stone office block in Blackwall Lane.

COMPLEX SUGARS

Following the closure of the soap factory, the site was taken over by Tunnel Refineries in 1934. This was formed on the basis of the Belgian firm Callebaut Freres et Lejeune in Aalst 1873. They wanted to manufacture glucose syrup to bypass taxes on sugar.

The Callebaut family remained influential until the year 2000. Customers included Shore Rock Co of Blackpool and Bassets Liquorice Co. and by 1939 Tunnel Glucose was the third largest British producer of glucose.

In the Second World War part of the premises was used by Thermalloys for the smelting of manganese from ore. The glucose factory closed and did other work until in 1943, Glenvilles moved in processing, oils and fats

With the war over they went back to producing the glucose from starch but prospects appeared bleak and supplies were of doubtful quality. The company began milling its own starch from maize. Soon after Glucoseries Reunies was renamed Amylum

In 1957 they changed to milling their own maize and suction gear was installed on their jetty where American maize was offloaded from coasters bringing it in from Rotterdam. In 1969 the curved office building at the entrance was completed to designs by Dennis & Partners of Wimpole Street. Buildings were erected next to the River, for Glenvilles production of instant milk and an administration and canteen block was built on with a car park on the site of what had been Idenden Cottages. The great off-shore silos were, to quote Owen Hatherley: 'silos to make le Courbouiser weep with envy' - and with them new and extended suction gantries for faster off-loading to shift 100 tons per hour.

View from the River early 2000
(Photo thanks to Peter Luck)

From 1982 both maize and wheat for starch were used as the costs of American maize pushed the company towards wheat. Eventually maize was no longer used and the silos fell out of use as wheat was brought in by lorry from the company's own mill in Suffolk.

The production of grain neutral alcohol began at a new plant on the old Molassine site in 1992. This was the first all-new distillation plant in London since the Beefeater gin distillery was built in 1908.

Amylum had been interested in the locality: and had been founders of the Greenwich Waterfront Development Partnership and funded environmental projects including on the riverside. This all stopped with Tate and Lyle takeover in 2000. In 2007 they were in turn bought out by Syral, a subsidiary of a French conglomerate Tereos and in 2009 they closed the Tunnel works down.

One day a demolition crew arrived and removed everything. They gave no notice to anyone and set about demolishing the riverside structures. While prompt action by the Greenwich Council and the Port of London authority saved the jetties the silos went. Then they left, leaving the site empty and derelict for others clear.

BRITISH OXYGEN

British Oxygen was one of the few companies to move to Greenwich during the Second World War. It was yet another established company siting a depot in Greenwich.

The works was on a site to the North of Tunnel Avenue, redeveloped for housing in 1998. It probably covered some of the site previously used by the ammunition works.

British Oxygen was set up by the Brin brothers in 1887 in Westminster and Glasgow and went on to become a successful multi-national.

During the Great War period the trend towards riverside sites being taken up by wharfingers and river service industries continued. British and Foreign Wharf Ltd. took over Greig's Wharf – where the linseed crushing mill had been. United Ship Builders and Repairers Ltd moved onto Providence Wharf.

TUNNEL AVENUE DEPOT

A different sort of industry was involved at Tunnel Avenue Depot built by the Metropolitan Borough of Greenwich as their basic services department. The depot dates from the 1920s and local contractors were used to construct a rubbish disposal plant with a chimney. The original plan was to build a rubbish destructor plant and a loan was obtained from the London County Council. Later rubbish was taken down a raised road to the River and tipped off the jetty into barges, shifting, for example, over 17,000 tons of rubbish in 1948. The jetty, built by Concrete Piling Co. in 1926 still stands but the road has gone.

A small building which still stands on site was a bathing centre – partly for the elderly but also with special facilities for 'verminous persons'.

Tunnel Avenue Disinfection building
(Photo thanks to John Kennett)

The depot was closed along with others with the opening of the large depot at Birchmere. The site is now in other use but some buildings remain.

NATIONAL BENZOLE

The site previously used for tar products continued in the early 1950s with another tar derivative– National Benzole. We have rather forgotten that petrol did not always come in tankers and pipes from the Middle East – some of it came from gasworks. National Benzole was owned by Shell and later branded as National, and ceased to be sold in the 1990s.

This is described as a storage facility and there is no reason to think this was not so. However, during the 1930s Coalene – 'British Coal Petrol' developed in Hackney by Carless, Capel and Leonard was produced at a carbonisation plant in Greenwich and sold to the RAF for use in fighter planes and also at roadside pumps. Clearly the adjacent huge gas works site and the Fuel Research Establishment must have had some role in this. But where the plant was we do not know.

Increasingly Greenwich wharves were used for riverside services, storage and warehouses, or for aggregates.

For instance in 1927 Eastwoods, the wharfage and brick making company, were situated on Greig's Wharf. They were a famous river haulage company dating from 1815 and through the early 19th century managed by Jane Eastwood. They had a brickworks at Shoeburyness and had a fleet of fifty sailing barges. Greenwich was one of several depots.

Tilbury Dredging and Contracting are a large Thames company with several depots up and down the River, providing services to river users and river maintenance. In 1906 they opened a depot in Banning Street next to Pipers apparently growing out of the previous Hughes barge repair business. From lighterage in the 1890s it has grown into the multinational, Interserve.

AGGREGATES

In the 1980s many of the wharves began to handle aggregates. When Delta Metal closed in the 1970s the site was taken by Civil and Marine - which specialised in sea dredged aggregates. At that time they operated two 5,000-ton sand and gravel dredgers from a headquarters in Purfleet. In 1995 they were bought by the Hanson Group and at that time had a bulk carrier and four dredgers.

As increasingly wharves are sites for blocks of flats so industry and its jobs has gone. The environment becomes more important. The gasworks vast site has been 'remediated; and other sites looked at with suspicion. The Blackwall Tunnel Approach is a source of great worry on air pollution and it has been the main platform for residents' campaigns against the proposed Enderby cruise line terminal and the Silvertown Tunnel and its approach. Pollution has always been with us

UNITED LAMP BLACK

The United Lamp Black Works was situated in the middle of the Peninsula. In 1930 ten inhabitants of Tunnel Avenue forced an action against pollution caused by this factory – and at the same time implied that Greenwich Council was negligent, despite surveys by the Sanitary Inspector over a period of ten years.

Mr. Webb had a 'dining rooms' at 159 Tunnel Avenue and he complained of the black specks coming from the factory. He pointed out that fans and ventilators at the factory were defective. He described how he made pastry for a steak pudding and found it full of specks. Customers who tried to eat the pudding, said ' *Hi Governor. What do you call this? Got a sweep knocking about here?*' [39]

DEVELOPMENT AND THE DOME

So what happened in the 20th century? To start with, in the period of the Great War and in the 1920s and 1930s industry continued to grow, some large works moved in, the River was used for haulage and many riverside sites went over to warehousing and transhipment.

By the end of the Second World War Greenwich Marsh was much more settled. There was a community there – in fact the local council electoral ward was called 'Marsh Ward'. There were numerous small houses around the area, many not of good quality and all of them built on damp marshland. Nevertheless a community had grown up.

In the late 19th century there had been a religious organisation in the form of the Mission to Seamen which was based on board a ship off Bugsby's Causeway and which had also met at rooms above a shop in Ceylon Place. This eventually moved to Gravesend and the little riverside church of St.Andrew.

There was a church in Blackwall Lane –. St Andrews which had been built 1900-2 replacing an 'iron church' partly funded with money from the demolition and sale of St Michael's, Wood Street, in the City. It had a pretty iron bell tower which is said to have come from the City church and which disappeared. St Andrews was demolished in 1984. There was also a Congregational church at Rothbury Hall, funded by the arms manufacturer Josiah Vavasseur. This pretty building remains and is now home to an arts project.

Dreadnought School was built by the London School Board School and may be from the late 1880s - since there are records of repairs and extensions in 1900.It closed as the population moved from the area in the 1960s and has been used as a store for the Horniman Museum ever since

There were social activities around the Co-partnership Institute in the gasworks where there was a theatre, and other social facilities. There were also playing fields with the huge gasworks sports club on the site now covered by IKEA. There were also allotments on the gas works sports field, and elsewhere.

PLANNING AFTER THE SECOND WORLD WAR

For planning after the Second World War the London County Council was guided by the Forshaw and Abercrombie Plan. In this Greenwich Marsh is coloured very clearly in red for industry. A programme began of clearance of housing from the area – it was marshy, unhealthy, the industry was polluting and noisy. Better to move the people out to quality housing which Greenwich Council and the London County Council were building on estates to the south.

I think it is very likely that in the 1940s and 50s people would not have understood what de-industrialisation was about. They would not have grasped that within the next fifty years this whole world would have changed. Maybe they thought industry should move out of London to green fields and life in new towns. Maybe they wanted to clean up areas like Greenwich Marsh – but for it to go completely would have been unthinkable. This was the world of the march of progress and 'Export or Die'.

A great deal has been written about redevelopment in Docklands and the area north of the River but Greenwich has had a lot less attention. As in Docklands there were many consultations and commissioned reports and one day someone should go through them to write a proper history. I am afraid that what follows is a ragbag of my recollections of what happened as regeneration loomed.

In 1973 Travers Morgan produced a report on the future of what was becoming called London Docklands; it had been commissioned by the Government. It addressed the changes which were clearly coming in the operation of the upstream docks. Containerisation in particular was going to change the pattern of riverside East London.

There is no space here- or time – to go through the many reports and studies. The Urban Development plans, the Urban Aid, the myriad regional planning bodies, the partnerships, the corporations and the constant changes in policies.

Briefly, Greenwich Peninsula was at first included in a new regional planning framework set up under what had become the Greater London Council. This was the Joint Docklands Committee and it worked with local consultees to produce a plan. The incoming Thatcher government changed all that. They set up the London Docklands Development Corporation and Greenwich was out of that. I have always understood that the motorway running down the centre of the Peninsula was seen as the drawback to future development – hence Greenwich Peninsula was not to be regenerated. However, Greenwich Council kept their autonomy and their planning powers but lost the cash.

North of the River and in Rotherhithe developers bought up sites from sometimes failing industries and built 'luxury' riverside housing, and an international business centre was added. Partnership bodies were set up to get more of this done outside the control of local authorities accountable to an often critical local population.

Greenwich continued to look at the future of the Peninsula as industries moved out and even the gas works was due to close. Community consultation meetings were held, there were aspirations and plans were drawn up. Local people wanted housing – nice three bed houses with gardens, and jobs – saying 'Tunnel Avenue jobs for Tunnel Avenue people'.

Eventually cash came in the form of small sums from various government bodies - but on the Peninsula industries closed. The gas works, the power station, the steel works were all large sites which became empty and on the site of the gas works a small forest sprang up. Gas by then was coming from the North Sea and the industry's plan for these large gas manufacturing sites was to mothball them. When the North Sea ran out then gas would be made again, so let nature move in until we need them. 'Let's keep the trees' some locals said. Some people had seen kingfishers as natural water courses reappeared.

Alcatel, Telcon's successor, continued as did the glucose refinery and many other smaller firms. Aggregate transhipment became a big thing. But factory after factory closed in Woolwich and Charlton until, in the late 1980s, Greenwich had the highest level of unemployment in the country.

As the riverside sites north of the River and in central London went over to housing and wharves closed so traditional riverside activity began to end. The construction of the Jubilee Line in Central London led to some panic because it was realised that there was nowhere through which spoil could be removed from building sites by river. The important sites used for basic facilities were being closed. As a panic measure a number of the wharves that remained open were 'safeguarded' which meant they must continue to be used for river activities. The biggest concentration of these was on the Greenwich Peninsula. Some have since been released for building house building purposes – for instance the site now known as The River Gardens. The safeguarding measure had been badly thought out and the wharves had been chosen because they were still in use rather than their suitability. There was also a problem in that boat repair yards and small boat building facilities were not safeguarded, leading to another crisis when it was realised that there was a lack of boat repair facilities on the Thames.

The push was to get some form of public transport to the Peninsula and there were lots of plans. An underground station had been proposed in the Morgan Stanley 1973 report as part of a proposal called the Fleet Line. This was later developed as the

Jubilee Line. The plan waited and waited until Olympia and York who were developing Canary Wharf in Docklands agreed with the Thatcher government a plan to finance it. This did not at first include an extension to Greenwich and many arguments followed as transport planners indicated that they thought an extension to Greenwich would be useless. The need for run-off tunnels beyond Canary Wharf meant that under-river tunnels would be built anyway and so it was eventually agreed to put shaft in at North Greenwich.

THEN CAME THE DOME.

Greenwich Council had tried and tried to bring in money to develop the area and at last here was a way. It seemed natural that Greenwich – known as 'the home of time' should use some of the vast empty spaces to house an exhibition, an echo of the 1851 Crystal Palace Exhibition and the 1951 Festival of Britain.. It also became clear that the gas works site would need extensive remediation and work began on that. The scheme was originally conceived by a Tory Government and the incoming Labour Government ummed and ahhed a bit about the exhibition plans. As the final decision was made Greenwich's Deputy Council leader Bob Harris, appeared on TV in his pink boiler suit – the sections of the Dome were on barges down the River, he said, will they come in, or not? The Government said 'yes'.

The Dome's architect, Mike Davies, wore a red boiler suit and the Dome rose up in front of us while being enthusiastically denigrated by the Press. It had echoes of the 1951 Festival in the designs which replicate the Skylon and the shape of the Dome of Discovery. It was all going to be very high tech and modern and there must be no mention of the past. Local firms couldn't get in – even Alcatel with their very high tech and very modern factory were not admitted because they were nasty old industry,

Finally there was money for a large architect designed station at North Greenwich on the Jubilee Line. In fact what we got was one of the largest stations built on the line at all. A sensible solution would have been to extend it to meet the South Eastern Railway lines at Charlton but even in 2000 this was unthinkable. A bus station was included in the design of the new underground station and numbers of buses began to end at North Greenwich. Suddenly the area was connected to the rest of South London although the only bus through the Blackwall Tunnel to North London continued to be the 108. A guided bus was planned from Charlton station to the Dome but that did not work and the track was used until very recently by ordinary bus routes. It proved very dangerous and there were several fatalities.

Early construction work on the Dome
(Thanks LB Greenwich Building Control Dept.)

There was however a special bus service for the Millennium exhibition run to the Dome from Charlton and Greenwich stations. This proved popular and was very much used by local people as frequent and convenient. It continued to run after the closure of the Dome in 2001. It was then discovered by the national press which ran a campaign about this 'ghost bus' and it was quickly removed and this useful and popular service was lost. The clipper service has also been a success. The boats run from the pier to Central London, thus taking commuters to and fro and visitors to events in the Dome and back. Going to London by Clipper means a seat and a cup of coffee.

There was also a plan for a Riverside tram route which would have come from Thamesmead and the route was safeguarded. However the route from the Dover to Cutty Sark was never defined and would have proved very difficult without the demolition of some popular and high quality housing. It was never built and eventually cancelled by Boris Johnson as London Mayor

Basically the New Millennium Experience Company redesigned the Peninsula – or at least the bits of it which they had acquired from British Gas, which included the steel works and the power station sites. The Morden College owned sites on the west bank were not included. Thanks to English Heritage the cottages at Ceylon Place were spot listed when I uncovered their actual date of construction. Apart from that everything old was swept away and landscaped with all the old field boundaries ignored. Where the tide mill ponds had been a hill was raised. Riverway no longer went to the River. Jetties and causeways were removed –including the historic causeway to Bugsby's Hole. We did get some art works – the Gormley statue by the Pier – Quantum Cloud - was installed then as was the Slice of Reality – the half boat round the back of the Dome.

The forest on the old gas works site was swept away and the resident foxes were driven out and there were stories of how they had been cemented into their underground dens to die there. The growing local green and ecology movement was unhappy with much of this. Green enthusiasts produced a report called 'Millennium Domesday' which outlined how very differently things could be done to preserve nature rather than to kill it. Some allegedly environmentally friendly facilities were included in the Dome project but few of them lasted very long

The Yacht Club was removed from its premises in the old Redpath Brown canteen and given a super new building and facilities – better than their wildest dreams. This was out in the River on Peartree Wharf and they have never looked back.

Ducks at the Ecology Centre

A hut was built for a future Ecology Centre. A water system put in for this proposed project, with some irony since this was a flooded marsh – a nearby site had been 'the goose pool' yet the abundant ground water could not be used. The ecology centre was eventually staffed and has been a great success and an ornament to the area.

Soon after the millennium exhibition opened I was elected as one of the local councillors for the area. This did not mean that I was catapulted into a world of decision making or even given any information about what was going on. The role of a local backbench councillor is not to be invited to parties or glamorous openings or meet important visitors. You are there to listen to the grumbles of local people and to try and sort out problems caused by professionals who proceed to patronise you. Discretion forbids very much detail on any of this but I never visited the Dome, or anywhere else, in any capacity other than as an ordinary local resident.

Cutting the ribbon at Lovell's for a new stretch of riverside path

The first new housing appeared in then Greenwich Millennium Village, built by Countryside developers and advertised as an 'eco' village. There was also a school and a health centre from the start. The national press never let up all year in its criticism of the Dome and everything to do with it. But Greenwich people generally were proud of it and defended it when they could.

AND AFTER .... AND NOW

When the Millennium Exhibition closed we saw the vast empty spaces of the Dome. What was to happen to it? Various competitions were held and various bodies bid for it. This was interesting. Some of the would-be developers had little idea about Greenwich - asked how they intended to use the river they seemed unable to understand the question. Others were only too keen to tell us how wonderful their plans were 'we want you to know that our Chairman is the most wonderful human being in the world'.

The exhibition was nearly 20 years ago and the Peninsula is a different place. The Dome itself is still there as a major entertainment centre but seems to impact little on most local people although it does provide jobs. The Dome has many formulaic chain restaurants and more lately a set of shopping outlets. It's not really clear who uses them.

The area immediately south of the Dome has now largely been developed by Knight Dragon, the developer who took on much of the land at the northern end of the Peninsula. They have installed a busy arts programme and an entertainment complex which is primarily directed at Peninsula residents. In the same area Ravensbourne College had been set up. This is a development of what had been Bromley Art School and which has concentrated on the commercial applications of arts in the digital world. Its striking building has an external design based on the Pemrose tiling of Dr.Roger Pemrose.

A new power plant has been installed by Knight Dragon on a site south of

Bullet from a Shooting Star

the Dreadnought School, with a dramatic 'optic cloak' flue designed by Conrad Shawcross. This envelopes a low carbon energy centre that will power 15,000 new homes and creates a landmark. Previous developments had been set up with what were essentially district heating schemes based around low energy systems with varying degrees of success.

The main addition to public transport has been the cable car funded by the Emirate's Airline—it actually describes the cross river services as 'an airline'. It was installed under Boris Johnson as Mayor of London. It goes to the Royal Docks and is very underused since most people want to travel towards Canary Wharf and the City. It continues to function despite low numbers of passengers.

On the roads traffic proliferates and jams up on a road system which has barely changed since the 19th century. Additions of fast roads were designed to service the Dome in 2000 by providing emergency exit routes from it and connecting them to the Blackwall Tunnel Approach motorway. These are generally useless for local movements.

We now have plans which appear about to be implemented for a new tunnel which will branch from the existing motorway to the east. It will then go across the Peninsula on a safeguarded road and then under the River to the Victoria Dock and Silvertown. There has been a great deal of opposition to this locally on grounds of pollution from increased traffic.

A proposed cruise line terminal at Enderby Wharf was also opposed by local people on grounds of pollution. There were never any signs that it was ever going to be built and the site owners have since admitted that it is not going to happen.

Meanwhile more and more flats are built by more and more developers. The Millennium Village has expanded and extended and most of the promised facilities have never happened. Sites originally designated for sports and community facilities have now been built up with flats. A promised trading estate of workplace units in Peartree Way has also been replaced by more flats.

Greenwich Millennium Village

It is also interesting to see how the nature of developers and development is changing. Early Docklands development was sometimes undertaken by local builders and funded from sometimes dubious sources. This was replaced by volume house builders interested only in more and more housing units and nothing in the way of community facilities. The single tenure local authority housing estates of the 1960 were condemned but replaced with nothing very different except that these new flats were 'sold' not rented by the local authority – and often 'bought to let' by private individuals, sometimes from abroad. Pre-sales in the Far East were far from unknown. However the local authority insisted that developers allocate a proportion of flats to for social housing depending on the planning agreement. There has been considerable criticism of the way that developers have sometimes managed to avoid both the social housing allocation and the community facilities. It is therefore encouraging to see some developers emerging who have worked hard to create a community and to provide workplace and social facilities along with the housing.

The Morden College sites on the west bank have not been part of the plans for those areas which were in the New Millennium Experience Company's holdings and now mainly in the control of Knight Dragon. However these ex-industrial sites on the west bank have one by one been taken over by developers and flats have been built. First was the Lovell's Wharf site with Granite Wharf and Piper's, all now called The River Gardens. Following a community campaign these blocks were built lower than the developer originally intended. Enderby Wharf has been developed with more flats following the demise and bankruptcy of the original developer.

Enderby House had become derelict following its sale to a developer and a lack of security on an adjoining site. Local people set up the Enderby Group to try and save it and to use it in some way tell the story of the telecommunications industry in Greenwich.

View from the (short lived) Enderby Sales Office
(Photo thanks to R.J.M.Carr)

It did not prove possible to persuade the developer to take any interest in this. Enderby House has now been refurbished and will become a public house. Another planned public house nearby was refused a licence and what appear to be attractive riverside sites for pubs may prove difficult given the lack of either public transport or any parking for private cars. An art work based on cable making called Lay Lines has been installed at Enderby Wharf.

Morden Wharf is now being redeveloped by a developer who has a reputation for community and arts focused regeneration. Beyond that Bay Wharf is now a busy working site with the boat repair business having moved there from Pipers and Badcock Wharves. Victoria Deep Water Wharf is still a safeguarded wharf and in use by Hanson who have recently installed a factory to manufacture various concrete structures. This has been very much welcomed by people in East Greenwich ands rather less enthusiastically by the new population of the Peninsula.

North of Hanson's most sites are owned by Knight Dragon who have taken an approach of installing facilities other than more and more flats. They have put in a considerable amount of community infrastructure albeit one aimed at a young population rather than one for families. Delta Wharf has a golf driving range which it is understood is only temporary and Point Wharf is being developed as an entertainment complex. Beyond that Ordnance Wharf now has an upmarket hotel.

Knight Dragon has also encouraged a plant and garden centre on the old power station jetty on the east bank following a project there for a theatre which never really took off. An earlier community project hoped to bring the historic boat collection to this area. The collection has however installed itself north of the river to Trinity Buoy Wharf and a ferry service across the river now runs to it from the pier by the Dome.

The Jetty built for the Power Station - it is now a gardening project

In the centre of the Peninsula our wonderful gas holder has been demolished because the Silvertown Tunnel builders wanted it down. It was an icon for the Peninsula from the River and from East Greenwich. Its demise is seen as a tragedy for the area which so badly needs something to give it identity.

The Peninsula and its new population are beginning to seem very separate from East Greenwich. There are people there who never come to Greenwich let alone go to Woolwich. Their whole focus is across the River to Canary Wharf where their jobs are. Many of these residents are transients and pre-Brexit there were many European or US nationals who had come here to work in the banking and commercial industries of the City and Canary Wharf. A surprising number of people have jobs in West London travelling on the Jubilee Line beyond Docklands. Many of these are looking to the Crossrail service when, and if ever, it opens to take them to jobs a great distance from their Peninsula homes. I was always surprised at the number of staff from major airlines living in Greenwich and going to work at Heathrow rather than City Airport.

Lay Lines by Bobby Lloyd

For centuries a path has gone along the Riverside along the top of the River wall. Greenwich people have always been very supportive of this and very angry at attempts to close it. There were several attempts to close it by industries in the late 19th century which were resisted with legal action by what was then the Greenwich vestry and supported by local people. As the Riverside has been developed for housing Greenwich Council has always insisted that the Riverside path be upgraded and remain open. This however was meant it is no longer a path along the river wall but a wide stretch of concrete divided into pedestrian and cycling tracks with willow and other large plants between it and the river. There have-been constant closures by developers and the Environment Agency in the name of safety and the need to enhance the path. This has been extremely unpopular with local people who are just as angry as those in the 19th century.

Enderby House dwarfed by the new flats behind it

In 1998 I published 'Greenwich Marsh' which was a brief history of the industries of the Peninsula. I had done my PhD thesis on the local gas industry and it seemed to be an easy project to complete. It was important because things were about to change so dramatically. We needed to tell the story of the past because it was being very much talked down by the builders of the Dome as old and dreary, dank and dark. I didn't think this was true – and also led to them sidelining the factory producing hi tech equipment for the net as 'old fashioned'. I later produced a condensed version of the first book called "Innovation Enterprise and Change on the Greenwich Peninsula' as an attempt to talk up the past and to put it into a context for the future.

Nothing exists in a void, even the future. We have to see how things develop and change in order to make sense of it. We do not have to see the past as bad in order to embrace the future.

The past remains with us, whatever we do. The popular view in the late 1990s says that pollution is, almost the only, legacy of past industry. Sorry, but pollution really isn't the point. The actual legacy is complex and much more relevant to the present than that. Going on about pollution - and nothing else - is in fact an insult to those who worked hard to leave us the world that we live in now.

This book has been an attempt to show how the Greenwich Peninsula developed and to suggest here that moving forward is not about rejecting the past. Greenwich is full of sites which pull the tourists in. Its working areas have been disregarded as mundane. I wanted to say that they have something to say to us too.

Nothing is old and romantic, but we live among the accretions of the past and we owe it some respect.

Steam tug Portwey and the now-demolished gasholder

NOTES AND REFERENCES

GREENWICH MARSH The quotation in the first paragraph is from Michael Baldwin, *The River and the Downs. Kent's Unsung Corner*. This is followed by reference to Nicholls, Cameron, Scaife, Stewart & Whitaker. *Bronze Age landscape of the Greenwich Peninsula*. Lambarde's Wall – now a particularly grisly side road is named for the Tudor Kentish historian, William Lambarde, once owner of this piece of land. 'Lea Ness' is shown on Robert Adams' map of Armada defences of 1588. The 'locals' who claimed to have Roman artefacts scavenged from the Dome site were staff at aggregate works. The Ghent connection is discussed in Julian Watson's article '*St.Peter's Abbey Ghent*' and the sites of its buildings on Ballast Quay are shown in *Greenwich Revealed* by Neil Rhind & Julian Watson. Manorial History was outlined by W.V.Bartlett in *The Industrial Development of Greenwich Marsh*. The 12th century tide mill is described by Damien Goodburn and Simon Davies, '*Two New Thames Tide Mills*' and it is understood that an updated version is pending.

THE MARSH SINCE 1315. Successive Marshland Commissioners and the laws that governed them are detailed in William Dugdale's 1662 *History of Imbanking and Drayning*. From 1625 administrative records of Greenwich Marsh are at the London Metropolitan Archive. A parallel archive from 1680 is at Morden College who have been major landowners here from that date. Early site ownership and occupation is detailed on the *Skinner Plan*. (1746)

THE SEA WALL . My articles on the rebuilding of the wall by Rennie are '*Breach in the Sea Wall*' (Bygone Kent) and *Greenwich Marsh Flood Defences* (Newcomen Bulletin). Detailed administrative records at London Metropolitan Archive and Morden College are extended here by reference to the City of London Thames Conservators records at the Museum in Docklands. The mud shute was owned by Flowers and Everett detailed in South Metropolitan Gas Co. Records in the National Grid Archive

EARLY BUILDINGS. The watch house is shown on Travers' plan of 1695 and Morden College deeds which include 'Watch House Field'. Morden College's 19th century housing was described by Michael Kerney '*Early Victorian Artisan Estate in East Greenwich*' and 1970s clearance plans by Greenwich Council in '*Housing in East Greenwich*' 1974.

OWNERSHIP OF THE MARSH. Greenwich Charities and their land holdings are described by Julian Watson in '*Some Greenwich Charities*'. Worshipful Company of Drapers, and Worshipful Company of Mercers, both have archive material on the sites. The Hatcliffe archive vanished in the 1970s. Poor of Farningham is thought to be a Roper family charity and a paper on this is held by Greenwich Heritage Trust. Morden College is, of course, a much larger concern both in terms of land holdings and activity. Their archive is an invaluable resource for Peninsula historians. There are also a number of histories of the College.

EARLY INDUSRY ON THE MARSH. Morden College's lease collection gives information on field leaseholds. Mr.Wheatley is described by Neil Rhind in *Blackheath Village and Environs*. The Tunnel Avenue haystack is shown in *Co-partnership Journal*, 1926 – and I rather suspect it is some sort of joke.

THE GOVERNMENT GUNPOWDER MAGAZINE. The magazine is included in Hogg's work on the Royal Arsenal where the site is not specified.

Peter Guillery wrote in the Newsletter of the, now defunct, Gunpowder Mills Study Group and a number of other articles followed by myself and Prof Alan Crocker. Hogg's reference and other material was buried in the, unindexed, Ordnance Department records at the PRO. Wayne Cocroft included further information in his *Dangerous Energy*. I have written a number of articles describing this depot in Bygone Kent, Greenwich Weekender and as part of a number of website based articles about Enderby Wharf. See below for details.

AN EARLY CHEMICAL INDUSTRY. Sites and references are taken from Morden College records and the St.Alfege poor rate records as well as Barbara Ludlow's work on *Coombe Farm*. There was a very large Deptford based copperas industry and the section is based on knowledge of this and the contemporary bleach industry as outlined by writers like Samuel Parkes (1839)

GIBBETS . The earliest reference to 'Bugsby' concerned the gibbeting of 'Williams the Pirate' and this involved research into his villainous career. The scale and the location of these grisly edifices was far from clear and I am grateful to Pieter van der Merwe for information and his article in a *Greenwich Society Newsletter*

BUGSBY. There has been a lot of speculation on reasons for the name 'Bugsby' – which dates from the early 18th century. I have also had correspondence from Dale Bugby in the US on his family background and it's relevant. Some details at https://greenwichpeninsulahistory.wordpress.com/?s=bugsby

DEVELOPMENT AT BUGSBY'S HOLE. The story of the East Greenwich Tide Mill has been a detailed piece of research culminating in a fully referenced article in London's Industrial Archaeology – following a more technical article by Brian Strong. I have repeated some of the story of the mill in a number of articles, listed below. Key documents were Gregory's *'Mechanics'* and the Sharpe v Russell Chancery judgment in the PRO.

THE REALLY, REALLY IMPORTANT ACCIDENT. I have used details of this accident, pivotal in the history of high pressure steam engines, in a number of articles listed below. Some details from Francis Trevithick's biography of his father, Richard Trevithick and from the contemporary press. Thanks to the late Rev.Dr.Richard Hills for extracts from the Watt papers. Further information from Southwark inquests in the City of London Record Office. Johnson's career can be traced through the patents. There is also a Wikipedia entry for is son, Cuthbert.

TROUBLE AT THE MILL. Maureen Greenhalgh drew my attention to Brian Donkin's diary in the Derbyshire Record Office which gives weekly and sometimes day to day instructions on remediation work.

DEVELOPERS. The history of the Marsh/Peninsula has effectively been that of a series of developments by landowners. Development in the 19th century was largely undertaken by Morden College and can be tracked in their records. Later, local authority and Government sources predominate

MORDEN COLLEGE AND THE EARLIEST DEVELOPMENTS. Clearly this chapter will involve a return to the Morden College archive and also the Ballast Quay website which gives source material and references http://www.ballastquay.com/ My articles for Greenwich Weekender - *The Men of Iron* (15/4/2020) and *Ballast Quay* (21/4/2020) also cover the area. George Smith and his career are covered by a Wikipedia biography

COLES CHILD. Coles Child inevitably features in the Morden College records. There is an article on him in relation to Bromley Palace by F.J. Filmer

COAL. Once again refer to the Morden College archive and to advertisements in the *Kentish Mercury* for sales of various types of coal locally. Sadly a specialist web site describing various chalk and gravel extraction sites in Greenwich has been deleted but the Spring 2020 edition of *Subterranea*, No. 53 5/2020 includes an article by David Whittaker's on *Mining and Quarrying at Maidenstone Hill* which covers some relevant sites

HOUSING. This is covered by Michael Kerney in *An Early Victorian artisan estate in East Greenwich* and in the Morden College archive

THE DURHAM COALFIELD. Street names are covered by Michael Kerney, below. It is also worth trawling the net for colliery names and associated web sites.

GREENWICH WHARF. Information based on the Morden College Archive and St.Alfege rate books helped by Neil Rhind's books on Blackheath residents. Some references in *Kentish Mercury*.

SHAW LOVELL. History of the firm by Eric Jorden, '*The story of Lovell's Shipping.*'

THE CRANES. Some information from Jorden, below. Thanks to Morris Cranes who tried very hard to identify the two cranes for us but were unable to do so because the licence plates had been stolen.

THE COAL TRADE. There appears to be surprisingly little written about this all important trade on London River. I wrote a brief article on the work of the *Greenwich Harbour Master* for Greenwich Weekender.

ENDERBY WHARF. The Wharf and its role in the history of cable making and telecoms is covered in detail in the enormous Atlantic cable web site. https://atlantic-cable.com/ Most of the works mentioned below in connection with the wharf are covered in it, frequently reproduced along with much much more. Thanks and congratulations to Bill Burns for this site.

ROPE. Information about Hounson from Government records (PRO) on the Woolwich rope walk. The saga about Mr. Littlewood is from press reports of his various trials. There are many books and much biographical material on the Enderby family – see Barbara Ludlow and Stewart Ash below, but there are several others. Description of the factory from the Greenwich Sewer records (LMA). The references to Faraday from press reports – but there are more details in recent collections of his letters. For details of Enderby House – see Enderby Group website, as well as the Atlantic cable site.

TELEGRAPH CABLES AT MORDEN WHARF. Details of this on the Atlantic cable web site – and special thanks to Stewart Ash for some detailed information on this site. Morden College archive, as ever, proved useful.

GLASS ELLIOTT AND THE MOVE TO ENDERBY WHARF. Most source material on this can be found on the Atlantic cable web site. There are also numerous books on the history of cable making in the run up to the successful Atlantic cable. Of specific local interest is Hill and Jeal's book specially written for Alcatel in 2000. Some others are listed below.

GREAT EASTERN. Brunel's great ship is the subject of many article and lectures which mainly cite her as a disaster – few, if any describe her brilliant successes. Many references to her and to the Atlantic cable can be found on the Atlantic Cable web site.

TRY AGAIN. Again – see the Atlantic Cable web site https://atlantic-cable.com/ . A small selection of some of the books and articles is included in the book list below.

TELCON AND ITS SUCCESSORS. Again – the Atlantic Cable web site details and reproduces numerous works about the site. *The Telcon Story* was published by the company in the 1950s and illustrates the works as a successful going concern. John Mackay and other cable ships were the subject of many works by artists in

the day – sadly not able to be reproduced here. There is a Wikipedia page about Charles Kao and a search of the net generally will turn up obituaries and tributes.
AND NOW. The Atlantic Cable web site does include a page of photographs of Enderby House and some details on its dereliction and restoration. The saga of the various developers, and indeed that of the cruise liner terminal, can be followed on the pages of Greenwich bloggers like 853 https://853.london/ and East Greenwich Residents https://www.egra.london/ and the source documents which can be unearthed on Greenwich Council's website planning pages.
AND THIS IS ALL ABOUT COAL TAR. My PhD was about the early gas indusr and the use of its residual products. I have thus always been acutely aware of the industries on the peninsula in the early 19th century which used coal tar as a raw material. I have been very tempted, in fact, to write a whole academiky article on it citing the Peninsula as a case history.
BRYAN AND HOWDEN. The main sources are the Morden College archive. I am however very grateful to Brian Sturt for information about their activities in building gas works and supplying equipment in Kent, Sussex and elsewhere.
CHARLES HOLCOMBE. Once more the Morden College archive has been invaluable. I am however also grateful to Georgina Green and information on her research on Valentines House and to a number of web sites concerning the Hatcham area, records from the Haberdashers Company and brewery history sites.
WILLIS AND WRIGHT. Once more the Morden College archive has been invaluable. I have also consulted web sites concerning the history of vinegar and the Champion family. I have however never really worked out why a prestigious vinegar manufacturer should take up the sale of naphtha.
JOHN BETHELL. I am rather aware of providing here a less than necessary account of this interesting man and his family. The whole history of wood preservation in the 19th century is important and moves on from some major work done on wooden ships. Once more the Morden College archive has been invaluable as have a number of web sites providing biographical information. Some specialist works – Lunge on *Coal Tar and Ammonia* have provided useful insights.
FRANK HILLS. Research on Frank Hills has been greatly helped by input from his family – in particular from his grandson, the late Patrick Hills – but also others. Clearly there is a great deal of interest in Frank's son, Arnold Hills in connection with West Ham Football Club and Thames Ironworks. I regret to say that minute books of Thames Ironworks during Frank's thirty years as Chair appear to be missing. I read my way through a vast archive of gas 19th century gas company minute books in London and some from the provinces. I could always rely on Frank to be there at some point - putting forward propositions which the gas companies couldn't refuse, despite suspecting, rightly, that they would end up losing. There is a large body of incomprehensible legal cases on patent rights (aimed at baffling the jury) and some mentions in the gas industry press of the day. I am also grateful to Brian Hope for showing me Hills' owned sites in Anglesey and North Wales – and to the Museum in Droitwich for Frank's activities in the salt industry and to the Museum in Huelva for his activities in Spain. I have found so much of this by accident – typically a local history publication will say how their important local chemical works was taken over by an unknown South London chemist. There is probably much, much more out there.
JOSHUA TAYLOR BEALE. This chapter is the result of years of work into Beale – starting with a file now with the Greenwich Heritage Trust. It is otherwise

compiled from contemporary magazines – *Mechanics Magazine* – and press reports. There is also a file in the Derbyshire Record Office. Thanks to Richard Albanese for advice and material on the rotary engine. Below are references to articles on Beale – but I am aware of inaccuracies in the older one which were corrected following later research.

APPLEBY BROTHERS. .This is based on information and an article by John Steeds who has researched the firm - and who I would like to thank. I am also grateful for information from Wagga Wagga.

AND IN THE BACK STREETS. The late Ted Barr provided GIHS with long lists of small back street engineering firms from his memories of the 1950s-60s. Information also from directories, rate books and Morden College.

BESSEMER. This, again, is based strongly on evidence from the Morden College Archive. Bessemer mentions his Greenwich works in his autobiography but it appears to have been ignored by subsequent biographers. Other information has come from rate books, the local press and chance notes in other sources. Information on Frederick Walton from Forbo Nairn archive. However – I am sure there is a lot more going on than has already turned up!

ALEXANDER THEOPHILUS BLAKELY. & THE CONNECTION WITH OPIUM. Blakely was an associate of Bessemer – and again there is probably a lot more going on here! In particular with relation to William Armstrong and his role at the Royal Arsenal. There are many US sources about Blakely guns and in Britain – I am grateful to staff at Fort Nelson for information and support. I wrote my original article on this with support from the late John Day and the late Adrian Caruna – and could not have done it without them. More recently there is an excellent biography of Blakely on the net by Steven Roberts. Research on the Dent family was in the archive at Kendal –where there are many boxes of records of activities in Greenwich.

THE WOODEN NUTMEG. A great deal of information here is from Barry's. *Dockyard Economy and Naval Power* published in 1863. There is also archive material on Nathan Thompson in the National Maritime Museum and at Mystic Seaport in Boston, US, who I would particularly like to thank. There is also material in the contemporary press.

MAUDSLAY, SON AND FIELD. I have used this material a great deal and have publications are listed below. This includes papers to a London Shipbuilders Conference and to a seminar at Kew Bridge Engines.

THE LADY DERBY. Much of this material comes from the local and national press – I am also very grateful to the late Hugh Lyon who provided information on ships built in the yard.

BLACKADDER. The saga of Blackadder's misfortunes is taken from Basil Lubbock's *China Clippers*. Reference has been made to material in the National Martime Museum – much of it focused on Cutty Sark – and numerous web sites which describe Willis and his ships. I would like to thank the Brazilian diving organisation who sent me photographs and information about her wreck. I note that there are now many other web sites about the wreck and that she is now a sight for toutrists.

HALLOWEEN. Halloween is also covered in works in the National Maritime Museum and on line. David Ramzam has covered Halloween in his *'Three Greenwich Built Ships'* albeit covering some aspects in more detail and from a different standpoint. I am grateful to the Devon diving organization that sent me photographs of her wreck, which is less well known than that of Blackadder. There was also considerable press coverage of her wrecking

THE TURKISH FERRIES. There are a vast number of web sites on these vessels, albeit they are in Turkish- but, along with Google Translate, they have been very helpful. I am grateful to a number of researchers who have written to me and who have tried to find what has happened to the hulk of Sahilbent.

THE LAST DAYS OF MAUDSLAY, SON AND FIELD IN GREENWICH. I must thank the late Hugh Lyon for providing names of many ships built in the yard and about the Belleville Boilers. Other information has come from the Morden College archive. The documentation on the final auction on the site is in the Science Museum library.

STOCKWELL AND LEWIS. . This is partly based on material in the South Met. Gas archive at National Grid Archive – and thanks to the staff there – and the House of Lords Enquiry into the building of East Greenwich Gas Works. Bulli is a diving site researched for the Tasmanian tourist authority – and thanks to them for information on her.

THE DRY DOCK AND WHAT HAPPENED TO IT & JOHN STEWART. This saga mainly comes from South Metropolitan Gas Company records at LMA and the National Grid archive. The capstan is, I hope, in the Museum in Docklands – I hope they have replaced the sign saying it came from Beckton Gas Works.

WILLIAM COURTNEY. This relies heavily on the Morden College arrive and some information in the Mercers Company archive. There is also some family history input

AND IN THE 20TH CENTURY. A surprising number of boats and small ships were built in the 20th century on the Peninsula. Only the building of the Dome and some enforcement methods seem to have deterred them. Records are very very hard to find.

SAILING BARGES. There are now many enthusiast groups and their web site for Thames sailing barges. This chapter was heavily dependent on information from Pat O'Driscoll and the late David Wood. There are innumerable essays on sailing barges – many by Pat – in short lived magazines and newsletters. More accessible are web sites: https://www.bargetrust.org/ https://sailingbargeassociation.co.uk/ .

BARGE BUILDERS BEFORE 1880 & CITY OF LONDON. Barge builders are very elusive and those before 1900ish even more so. The little we know comes from Morden College.

PIPERS. There is a lot of information out there about Pipers – from workers, and enthusiasts. I am sorry that no one from the family would talk to me. Several of their barges are famous – in particular Giralda whose picture appears on all sorts of unlikely items. Enthusiast web sites will give a lot of information

SHRUBSALL. As with Pipers there is information on enthusiast web sites and publications

NORTONS. I am grateful to Pat O'Driscoll who knew the yard well and worked there. There are also enthusiast and family history webs sites

THE LAST GREENWICH BUILT BARGE AFLOAT. See https://www.facebook.com/pg/SBOrinoco/ and research undertaken by Jim Hughes on Orinoco outlined in an article listed under my own publications

THE FIRST BRICKS. This comes from the minutes of the Greenwich Commission of Sewers together with research in local directories.

WINKFIELD BELL. Along with other cement works listed here material comes from Morden College archive and local directories. There have also been references to A.K. Francis, *The Cement Industry*, and the invaluable https://www.cementkilns.co.uk/
JABEZ HOLLICK – as above, plus reference to Neil Rhind's *Blackheath and its Environs*.
ASHBY – as above, plus some information from Staines – the now defunct museum was extremely helpful and sadly has been replaced by a library system which is very much less so.
SIR JOHN SCOTT-LILLIE. This comes from Morden College and local rate books. There is Wikipedia and other biographical information on line.
WILLIAM BUCKWELL. In addition to Morden College and the rate books there are numerous riveting press reports of his time in Italy, bail offences and bankruptcy. I have been unable to discover much about the railway he was allegedly building.
GRANITE WHARF – REAL STONE. Much of this piece comes from Swanage based literature including Lewer and Calkin, *Curiosities of Swanage*. I have also had some information from Stewart Borrett and the Swanage Museum. I would also like to thank Eric Robinson for information both written and verbal. Other information from Morden College archive and staff at the old Woodlands Local History Library.
PATENT STONE – STONE MANUFACTURED IN GREENWICH. Again information comes from the Morden College Archive and local rate books. I have to thank researchers from Ipswich on Ransoms and there are some contemporary technical press accounts. There are many websites about Ernest Leslie Ransome and his work in US – although none of them mention this Greenwich works that I am aware of.
THE GAS WORKS. East Greenwich was a very very important gas works although there is surprisingly little written about it. The South Metropolitan Gas Co. Minute books are in the London Metropolitan Archive, there is a small collection at the National Grid Archive in Warrington, and there may be something in unopened boxes at the National Gas Museum in Leicester. The company and the East Greenwich works are covered in great detail in the professional press – *Journal of Gas Lighting* and *Gas World*, and some other publications. The works was also covered in the company magazine '*Co-partnership Journal*'.
GEORGE LIVESEY. I am afraid I have a half written biography of Livesey still hidden on my laptop. Livesey dominated the gas industry in the late 9th century and there is a vast amount of information on him in the professional press of the day
THE GAS HOLDERS. The demolition of East Greenwich No.1 in 2020 has resulted in a rash of material on the web and elsewhere. The best information is either from Malcolm Tucker's unpublished report on London gasholders for English Heritage and Barbara Berger's *Der Gasbehälter als Bautypus* (in German). I have myself written so many short articles on it that I have actually forgotten most of them – some of them are listed below (they all say he same anyway). The larger and more advanced holder. East Greenwich No2 has been demolished in the 1980s. It had been badly damaged n the 1915 Silvertown Explosion. The picture below shows it being cleared after the explosion and reveals its immense size.

GREAT STRIKE OF 1889. My M.Phil in 1986 was about Labour Co-partnership under George Livesey and included a chapter on the so-called strike. It is a subject which has been very much misunderstood and interpreted via Will Thorne's very partisan biography. For a more informed view read Derek Matthews 1985 PhD Thesis from Hull on the *London Gas Industry*.
CO-PARTNERSHIP. I would recommend my MPhil Thesis!
COLLIER SHIPS. There are many stirring tales and some terrible shipwrecks in successive issues of *Co-partnership Journal*. Brian Sturt has written a number of pieces on the fleet for Lewisham Local History Society and Historic Gas Times.
ORDNANCE TAR WORKS. I was given a huge archive of photographs and exhibition material by Faye Gould, widow of an ex-manager of the works. Brian Sturt has reproduced some of these with commentary in *Historic Gas Times*. I also showed them to an extremely appreciative audience at a meeting of gas historians in Manchester.
PHOENIX WHARF. There are numerous TV thrillers from the 1970s and 1980s which were filmed in this area. I am afraid much of my investigations in the 1980s were whole in the fence episodes.
COALITE. Web sites and brochures on the Coalite Company
FUEL RESEARCH. There are details of this organisation in numerosus official report The now closed Plumstead Museum had a large archive of photographs which I assume are now with the Greenwich Heritage Trust.
WAR MEMORIAL This is now included in Greenwich Council's round of war memorial services.
THE GHOST. I really don't know what to say about this – but it was a lot of fun at the time, and got me on TV and on a river trip with all sorts of media persons.
LINSEED. Thanks to John Grieg for information.
ASBESTOS. History of Taylor and Newall *'The Way to Dusty Death'* by P.Bartrip
SOAP. Most of this comes from websites and from Morden College. Also Peter Luck's *'Sugar and Soap'* published on the GIHS web site. Enquiris to the Unilever

Arhive reslted in very little. Information on the Soames family from Neil Rhind's *'Blackheath and its Environs'*.

FORBES ABBOTT. Information from chemical industry archive material concentrates on their Old Ford site. Thanks to Faye Gould for pictures and information.

BIPHOSPHATED GUANO & MOCKFORDS. Details from the Morden College archive plus works on pollution by E.Ballard.

BRIQUETTES. Details from Morden College and family history web sites on Wylam.

PERCIVAL PARSONS. Thanks to Neil Rhind who has researched Mr. Parsons There is web site information on Manganese Bronze.

THOMAS ROBSON. Greenwich Rate Books and map information. The story .of the explosion is taken from *Kentish Mercury* and by the official accident reports of Vivian Majendie.

HOUSES. The Booth Report is invaluable as is Barbara Ludlow' article *'Social Conditions on Greenwich Marsh*. The flat above the Tunnel gatehouse s detailed in the Hisrtoric England listings report. .

EAST LODGE. Thanks to Maj Wagstaff for information on the Davies family amd copies of *'The Four Wheeler*. There are also interviews with them reported by *Kentish Mercury*, Jamet Hewes is covered in a series of newspaper articles on various legal actions and his eventual suicide. There are web based records of the yachting organisations.

CUTTY SARK TAVERN. There is an excellent history of the Tavern by Neil Rhind on the Ballast Quay web site.

SALUTION. Shown on Morden College Survey plan from around 1800

SEA WITCH.& other pubs listed. Information in Morden College archive and thanks to Stewart Ash for additional information.

THE MITRE. Mentioned in South Met. Minutes. Most of this is from my own memory .

SHIP & BILLETT – and GREENWICH TOWN SOCIAL CLUB. Web site information plus my own memories.

MEANTIME. From their website

ANGERSTEIN RAILWAY. There are a number of articles on the railway listed below.

THE DOCK THAT NEVER WAS. This is taken from many reports in issues of the *Kentish Mercury*. Interpretive drawing by Chris Graham, with thanks,

BLACKWALL TUNNEL. This is taken from innumerable web sites on the tunnel plus a summary of the works prepared by Francis Ward for Greenwich Council on its centenary. There is also information and references in the Historic England listings report and on the *Survey of London* volume on Poplar and the Isle of Dogs.

KNACKERS.. There is web site information on Harrison Barber.

ELECTRICITY. The archive of the electricity industry was destroyed when the industry was privatised and there are no records of Blackwall Point that I am aware of. Material comes from site visits, memories and an article on the older station in *Engineering.*

LINOLEUM.. Thanks to the Kirkaldy Museum for numerous items from the Forbo Nairn archive

VICTORIA DEEP. Articles in PLA Magazine

REDPATH BROWN. Thanks to Andrew Turner for information from his work and that of his father, Arthur. Also thanks to the late Rick Tisdall and his sister. Also thanks to staff at the Dorman Long museum
DELTA METAL. Thanks to Johnson and Phillips for sight of some of their archive material on Delta
MOLASSINE.. Thanks to many ex-workers who have given and shown me items from the factory and passed on their memories.
SUGAR. Again thanks to the many ex-workers from Amylum who have helped with this. Also reference to Peter Luck's *'Soap and Sugar'*. Photo by Peter Luck with thanks
BRITISH OXYGEN. Web site and memory information
TUNNEL AVENUE DEPOT. Records of the Metropolitan Borough of Greenwich.
UNITED LAMP BLACK. Local press reports.
FINAL section comes almost entirely from my own knowledge of what went on. From 1986-1998 I worked for Docklands Forum which monitored regeneration in Docklands on behalf of community groups. I prepared their monthly mail out and latterly researched the history of the organisation, which was published. From 2000-2014 I was the local London Borough of Greenwich Labour councillor for the local area and had a close-up view of what went on! I hope it is all reasonably accurate.

THANKS–.....to Elizabeth Wiggans, the Morden College archivist. Thanks to staff at the old Woodlands Local History Library – the late Barbara Ludlow who should have had the time to finish her research on the Enderbys and to Julian Watson who has put up with my queries since 1970 and has to continue to sort them out some fifteen years after he has retired. Thanks to Jacky Robinson who has proof read this, to Rob Powell for pictures and support, to Bob Carr and Pam Carr for pictures, support and technical explanations, and also Peter Luck and Leon Yohai for support and pictures. I have many more pictures which have not had space to use– from Greenwich Council Building Control Section, Southern Gas Networks, National Grid Archive, Morden College and many, many people who took stunning pictures of EGNo1. Holder being demolished.

And of course, thanks to my late husband, Alan Mills, for putting up with me at all.

217

FURTHER READING

Angerstein Wharf, Southern Railway Magazine, Dec1925 & Nov 1951
Ash, Stewart. The History of the Repeater. https://atlantic-cable.com/
Ash, Stewart. The Eponymous Enderbys. https://atlantic-cable.com/
Ash, Stewart. The Story of Subsea Telecommunications & its Association with Enderby House. https://atlantic-cable.com/
Ash, Stewart. The Cable King, - Sir John Pender. 2018 Amazon
Baldwin, Michael . The River and the Downs. Kent's Unsung Corner
Ballard.E. Report on the Lower Thames 1871
Barry, P. Dockyard Economy and Naval Power. London, 1863
Bartlett, W. V. The Industrial Development of Greenwich Marsh'. Trans G&LAS. 1966
Bartrip, P. The Way to Dusty Death'.
Berger, Barbara. Der Gasbehälter als Bautypus. Munich 2020
Bonwit, William. Leonard Searles the Elder and the Development of Blackheath Hill, Trans G&LAS 2 1980.
Carpenter. David .Dockland Apprentice
Carina, Adrian. Alexander Theophilus Blakely, Ordnance Society Journal. 4, 1992
Carr, Frank Sailing Barges, London, 1931,
Century of Gas in South London. S.Met. Gas Co. 1926
Cocroft, W. The Archaeology of Gunpowder and Military

Explosives Manufacture (English Heritage. English Heritage. 2000
Crocker, Glynis. Gunpowder mills gazetteer. Gunpowder Mills Study Group. Soc. Protection of Ancient Buildings, 1988
Cunnane, Berni. Carving out history. The regeneration of the Enderby Wharf Ferry Steps https://atlantic-cable.com/
Day, Karen. Searching for Hoskins GIHS blog
East Greenwich Gas Works' Archive, No.1. March 1994.
Filmer, J.L Bromley Palace and Coles Child, Lord of the Manor of Bromley. 1846-1873, Bromley Local History. 5, 1980
First Greenwich Power Station. https://greenwichindustrialhistory.blogspot.com/2016/11/the-first-power-station-on-peninsula.html
Francis, A.K. The Cement Industry 1796-1914,
Gas Works Shipping Dept. GIHS blog
Green Allan .lit all started in Ireland
Green, Allan. 150 Years Of Industry & Enterprise at Enderby's Wharf. https://atlantic-cable.com/
Green, Allan. Dark side of former Wonder Material GIHS blog
Green, Allan. Last monument t Britain' Subsea Cables
Greenland, Maureen & Day, Russ. Brian Donkin. The Very Civil Engineer. 2016
Guillery, Peter & Pattison, P. The powder magazine at Purfleet, Georgian Group Journal, VI
Gunpowder Mills Study Group Newsletter 19 August 1996, Wayne Cocroft comments

Gunpowder Mills Study Group Newsletter 25, October 1998 note by Peter Jenkins
Gunpowder Mills Study Group Newsletter No.21 August 1997. Mary Mills. Critique
Gunpowder Mills Study Group Newsletter No.22 June 1998. Alan Crocker – Review
Hill & Jeal Greenwich – Centre For Global Telecommunications Since 1850. Alcatel. 2000
Hill, Ed. Eyesore proposal for Greenwich Peninsula
Hilton, John. Mr. Angerstein's Railway. Bygone Kent, Vol.20 No.2. February 1999.
Hogg, Oliver. The Royal Arsenal, Vol.1. OUP, 1963.
Housing in East Greenwich. LBG Report No.2. Directorate Housing Services 11/ 1974
How it was first achieved. Wonders of World Engineering 1938.
Jenkinson, Sally. The Enderby Family of Enderby Wharf
Jenkinson, Sally. Development of the Telegraph
John Julius Angerstein and Woodlands, Woodlands Art Gallery, 1974.
Jordan, Eric, The story of Lovell's Shipping.1992
Joyce, Patrick . Patronage and Poverty in Merchant Society. A History of Morden College
Jubilee Geological Wall at Watchet Station. Leaflet
Kentley, Eric & Halse, Robert. Brunel's Great Eastern. Brunel Museum.
Kerney.Michael. An Early Victorian artisan estate in East Greenwich. Trans G&LS Vol IX No.6 1984
Lewer, David and Calkin, J.Bernard, Curiosities of Swanage or Old London by the Sea, Dorchester, 1971.

Linney, A.G. Harbour Master's House. Co-partnership Journal 1910
Lubbock, Basil. The China Clippers. Glasgow. 1914
Luck, Peter. Sugar and Soap. https://greenwichindustrialhistory. blogspot.com/2015/01/soap-and-syrup-peter-luck.html
Ludlow, Barbara. Early History of Coombe Farm.
Ludlow, Barbara. 'Social Conditions on Greenwich Marsh 1837-1901', Trans. G&LAS, Vol. VII, No.3. 1968.
Ludlow. Barbara Whaling for Oil. The rise and fall of the Enterprising Enderbys. GHS Vol.3 Nos 3&4
Lunge, G. Coal Tar and Ammonia, 1909
Merwe. Pieter van der. The Greenwich Gibbets. Greenwich Society Newsletter. 11/2018
Millichip, East Greenwich Gas Works Railway. Railway Byelines 11/1998
Morris, P. Archives of the Chemical Industry, BHSS, 1988.
Nicholls, Cameron, Scaife, Stewart & Whitaker. The Bronze Age landscape of the Greenwich Peninsula. London Archaeologist. Vol 14 No11 Winter 2017
Parkes, S. Elementary Treatise on Chemistry, London, 1839
Perks, Richard-Hugh 'The Barges of Frederick Hughes of East Greenwich' Bygone Kent, February 2001
Ramzam. David C. Three Greenwich Built Ships. Amberley 2013
Rhind. Neil Blackheath Village and Environs 1790-1970. Vol.1. Blackheath
Riddle, David. Alcatel. GIHS blog
Roberts, Bob.. Coasting Bargemaster

Roberts, Steven. Captain Alexander Blakely RA. https://www.scribd.com/document/97550420/Captain-Alexander-Blakely-RA
Smith, R. Sea Coal for London
Steele, Jess. The Streets of London. The Booth Notebooks. South East.
Strong, B. A Tidal Mill at East Greenwich. London's Industrial Archaeology No.13
Sturt, Brian. Low Pressure Gas Storage, London's Industrial Archaeology, No.2. 1980
Sturt, Brian. George Livesey's Ghost. Greater London Industrial Archaeology Newsletter 178 Oct. 1998
Tadman. Julie A Fisherman of Greenwich
Telcon Story. Telcon
Transatlantic Telecommunications timeline. GIHS blog
Turner, Andrew. Redpath Brown GIHS blog
Watson, Julian, Some Greenwich Charities. Trans G&LAS, Vol. VIII, No.3. 1975.
Watson, Julian & Rhind, Neil. Greenwich Revealed. Blackheath Society 2013.

Watson, Julian. St.Peter's Abbey Ghent. Jnl Greenwich Historical Society 3/6 2009.
West, Jenny. Gunpowder, Government and War in the Mid-Nineteenth Century. Royal Historical Society Studies in History 63, 1991
Whittaker, D. Mining and Quarrying at Maidenstone Hill. Subterranea, No. 53 5/2020
Wood, David and Elizabeth The Last Berth of a Sailorman.
Greenwich Industrial History blog – articles on Greenwich Industrial History since 1998. Many about the Peninsula and its History. http://greenwichindustrialhistory.blogspot.com/
Greenwich Peninsula History blog – articles and reproduced original documents on a wide range of industries and institutions on the Greenwich peninsula https://greenwichpeninsulahistory.wordpress.com/
Greenwich Industrial History Facebook page – shorter items and reviews. Many about Peninsula history https://www.facebook.com/groups/1549240565122658/

Mary Mills –Works on Peninsula History

Alexander Theophilus Blakeley. Ordnance Jnal 2001
Beale's Gas Exhauster. Greenwich Weekender 10 June 2020
Bessemer and Greenwich. GLIAS Newsletter. Letter
Blackadder. Greenwich Visitor.

Blackwall Point Greenwich Society Newsletter Sept/Oct2018.
Breach in the Sea Wall, Bygone Kent. 19/.4.
Bugsby's Reach http://onthethames.net/2014/02/

14/platform-defence-bugsbys-reach/
Bugsby's Reach consultation. GLIAS Newsletter
Case for listing cranes at Lovells Wharf Groundwork 1999
Ceylon Place cottages. Greenwich Visitor
Damn Your Eyes Mr. Sharp. Meridian Mag. March 2000
Dock That Never Was, Bygone Kent . 20/.4
Drugs, Guns and High Finance. Bygone Kent. 19/7.
Early Gas Industry and its Residual Products in East London. M. Wright 1994
East Greenwich Gas Holder is going. Newcomen Links. Sept 2019
East Greenwich No.2. GLIAS Newsletter 1986
East Greenwich Tide Mill London's Industrial Archaeology 17. 2019
Enderby Leaflet (with Stewart Ash)
Enderby Wharf. The True Story. Westcombe News Feb 2017 (with Peter Luck)
Explosion at Blackwall Point. Greenwich Weekender 5th September 2018
Explosion 200 years ago. Industrial Heritage. Vol. 32 Winter 2007
Explosive magazine at Greenwich Weekender 17th June 2020
Explosive Magazine at Greenwich. Bygone Kent, 18/12.
Finding the Bulli. GIHS Newsletter Vol.2/ 5
From Greenwich across the Atlantic. G'nwch Wknder 16th July 2020
From Mr Bugsby to the Coaling Jetty. Booklet
From the Great Meadow to the Barge Builders Greenwich Weekender 27 May 2020

Gas Workers Strike in South London. South London Record 4, 1989.
George Livesey Business History 1988
Georgian Cottages on the New Millennium Experience Site
Georgian Cottages nearly demolished for the Millennium Exhibition. Greenwich Soc. Newsletter
Docklands Forum; GIHS April 1998
Give 'em enough Rope Greenwich Weekender. 24 June 2020
Granite Wharf. Greenwich Weekender. 13 May 2020
Greenwich and Woolwich at Work Suttons 2002
Greenwich Gunpowder Depot, Gunpowder Mills Study Group, 21.
Greenwich Harbour Master. Greenwich Weekender. 16th May 2018
Greenwich Inland Linoleum, Bygone Kent, 20/3.
Greenwich Marsh Flood Defences. Newcomen Bulletin 170, April 1998.
Greenwich Marsh, M.Wright 1999
Greenwich Peninsula. Docklands Forum 1999
Greenwich ships travelled far. Greenwich Weekender 10th June 2019
Gunpowder Inspection and Death. Bygone Kent. 19/l.
Henry VIII King of Industrial England. Greenwich Visitor November 2018
Henry Bessemer in Greenwich. Newcomen Soc Bulletin, 172, 1998.
Hills Family, Bygone Kent, 18/3,
History of the Holder Greenwich Weekender. 16th April 2018
How I found the Dry Dock Capstan. Greenwich Weekender 23rd April 2019

How Time and Tide shaped our History. Greenwich Visitor Oct. 2008
Ice Well at Lovells Wharf Kent Underground Research Newsletter.63
Industrial Accident at East Greenwich. Bygone Kent, 17/11, 1996
Industrial Site in East Greenwich. Bygone Kent, 17/12 1996.
Innovation, Enterprise and Change on the Greenwich Peninsula. 2018
Into the Marshland. Greenwich Weekender. 29th April 2020
Jetty. Booklet 2018
Jim Hughes and Orinoco Bygone Kent February 2001
John Beale and Joshua Beale, Inventors from Greenwich Marsh, Bygone Kent, 18/6, June 1997
John Beale of Greenwich. Industrial Heritage. Vol 28 Summer 2002
Jumbo. No More, Greenwich Soc. Newsletter
Kicking up a right stink G'nwch Wknder 13 March 2019
Looming against the sky is the skeleton of the great holder. Greenwich Weekender. 8th Aug. 2019
Lovell's Wharf. Booklet
Lovells Wharf. Bygone Kent. Nov & Dec. 1999 & March 2000
Made in Greenwich. *The Appleby Beam Engine.* Greenwich Soc. Newsletter
Man *who laid cables under Atlantic.* Greenwich Weekender. 13 June 2018
Maudslay Son and Field for Kew Bridge Engines Trust CD 2002
Maudslay, Son and Field in Greenwich. Bygone Kent. In three parts Jan, Feb & March 2002
Medieval tide mill Greenwich Weekender. 6th May 2020

Memorial to the dead in the Great War from the East Greenwich Gasworks. Greenwich Soc. Newsletter
Millennium Site - Bad Smells on Greenwich Marsh, Bygone Kent, 17/7 July 1996.
Millennium Site - Who built the Gas Works, Bygone Kent, 17/5, May 1996.
Millennium Site, New East Greenwich, Bygone Kent, 17/8 1996,
Molassine. Bygone Kent
Molassine Co. & smell to remember. G'nwch Wknder 8th June 2019
Mystery Steel Works, By'ge Kent. 20.
Nathan Thompson and the Wooden Nutmeg. Bygone Kent. 19/ 5.
Olinthus Gregory. Description of the East Greenwich Tide Mill. Industrial Heritage Vol.33 Spring 2007
Our Poor Doomed Gas Holder G'nwch Wknder 6th March 2019
River People G'nwch Wknder 3rd June 2020
Shipbuilding in East Greenwich. Thames Shipbuilding Study Group
Stockwell and Lewis. Dry Dock Bygone Kent 20/9.
Tragic death of Mary Mahoney killed on her first day at the firework factory. G'nwch Wknder 6th December 2017
Tragic demolition of Jumbo. Greenwich Soc. Newsletter
Thames Tunnels. AIA Newsletter 140. Spring 2017
We made History on an Industrial Scale. Greenwich Visitor Sept. 2018
Writing the History of the Greenwich Peninsula. OU Student Journal

INDEX

108. bus, 171, 194
Acontyus, 9
AEC bus for Blackwall Tunnel, 171
Agamemnon, 46, 47
Aggregates, 178, 187, 92
Alcatel, 51, 192, 194
American Civil War, 77
ammonia salts, 65
Amylum, 140, 141, 156, 183, 184
Anchor Iron Wharf, 28, 154
Anderson, John, 122
Angerstein line, 134, 162 -166
Angerstein, John Julius, 162
Angerstein, William, 116, 164, 165
Anglesey, 62, 66
Antarctic exploration, 41
Anthracene, 142
Appleby Bros. 69-70
Armada defences, 207
Armoury mill, 16
Armstrong, William, 74, 76

Arnold's Sluice, 8
Artificial manure, 143
Artificial stone, 113
Asbestos, 139
Ashbridge, James, 72
Ashby, George Crowley, 115
Ashby, John, 34
Atlantic Telegraph, 45-49, 209
Atlantic Telegraph Company, 45
Auckland Islands, 42
Badcock's Wharf 31, 101, 110
Bahia, 88
Ballast, 27, 31
Ballast Quay, 7, 26-28, 37, 154, 161, 167, 207
Balsopps, 8
Band of Hope, 124, 130
Bank Place, 113
Bankruptcy sale, 94
Bankside, 55

Banning Street, 32, 111, 119, 145, 187
Barge builders, 103, 109, 110
Barge races, 105
Baring, Thomas, 78
Barlow, Thomas, 68
Barratt, 39
Basket maker, 15
Bay Wharf, 58, 81, 84, 101, 110, 112, 117, 202
Bazalgette, Joseph, 168
Beale, Joshua 64-66
Beale, Benjamin, 68, 69
Beale, John, 69
Bedlam's Bottom, 106, 109
Bell's Asbestos Company Ltd, 139
Belleville Boiler Works, 93
Bellot Street, 6, 72
Belvedere Wharf, 29
Bendish Marsh, 20
Bendish Sluice, 8
Bessemer, Henry 70 79, 121, 122, 145, 147, 157
Bethell, John, 57-59
Bethell's Cottages, 148
Bethell's Wharf, 176
Bicknell, John, 22, 113
Biggs, Reginald, 28
Binnie, Alexander, 169
Biphosphated Guano Co., 143
Blackadder, 83, 84, 86, 87, 88, 89
Blackheath, 28, 30
Blackheath and Greenwich Electric Light Co, 173
Blackwall Lane, 8, 12, 15, 27, 80, 129, 157, 158, 159, 160, 167, 173, 183, 189
Blackwall Point, 6, 8, 21, 60, 99, 126, 148, 173, 174
Blackwall Point Dry Dock, 99
Blackwall Point Power Station, 173, 174
Blackwall Tunnel, 27, 93, 99, 127, 149, 157, 158, 166-172, 178, 179, 188, 194, 199
Blackwall Tunnel Approach, 127
Blakeley Ordnance Works, 149 157
Blakely, Alexander Theophilus, 76, 79, 95-96, 132
Bleach, 19, 20, 155

Blenheim Engineering Co. 147
Board of Works Wharf, 31
Boat repair yards, 192
Booth, Charles, 148
Boreman Charity, 12
Bosporus ferry service, 90
Boulton and Watt, 24
Bow Creek, 6, 95
Braddyll Street 33
Brandram, 95
Brick making, 22, 32, 113
Brin brothers, 185
Briquettes, 117, 144
Bristol Steam Navigation, 35
British & Foreign Wharf Ltd., 185
British Gas, 195
British Oxygen, 185
Bromley by Bow, 62
Bromley, Kent, 30
Bronze Age, 6
Brunel, I.K. 46, 48, 169
Brunel, Marc, 84
Bryan and Howden, 56
Bryan, John, 55
Buckwell, W. 117
Bugby, 22
Bugbsy 20, 22
Bugsby's Causeway, 189
Bugsby's Hole, 21
Bulli, 96
Bullock, George, 104
Burt, Boulton and Haywood, 60
Burt, George, 118, 119
Bus station, 194
Butler, James William, 122
Butters' Crane, 35
Cable, 25, 39-52, 107, 114, 122, 199
Cable ships, 51
Cadet Place, 119
Callebaut Freres et Lejeune, 183
Caradoc and Usworth, 34
Caradoc Street, 32
Carpenter, Charles, 131
Carpenter, Dave, 171
Castillion, 9
Cat's Brains., 8
Cement manufacture, 34, 113, 114
Central Repair Depot, 166
Ceylon Place, 23, 148, 189, 195
Chalk pits, 30

Champion's Vinegar Brewery, 58
Charles Holcombe, 56, 57
Charlton Football Ground, 31
Chemical works, 132
Chester (le Street) Street, 32
Chester Station, 121
Child, William Coles, 29-34, 57, 58, 118, 126, 148, 164
Chiselhurst,, 28
Christchurch Way, 32
City of London, 13, 14, 40, 143, 162, 168
City of London Gas Company, 40
City of London, barge, 105
Civil and Marine, 187
Clipper service, 194
Coal, 30, 37, 54
Coal merchants, 34
Coal tar, 40, 54-60, 67, 116, 141, 144
Coal trade, 37, 124
Coalene, 187
Coalite, 134
Cockle's Reach, 21
Coke, 30, 31, 115, 134
Coke ovens, 30
Collier fleet,17, 30, 32, 37, 133-134, 161
Commerel Street, 111
Composition, 40, 116, 117
Computer system, 35
Congregational church, 189
Constable, John Archibald, 174
Co-operative movement, 130
Co-partnership, 129
Co-partnership Institute, 190
Copperas, 20
Corporation of the City of London, 10
Cory, William, 85
Countryside, developers 197
Courage's Brewery, 158
Court of Sewers, 8, 9, 10
Courtney, William, 100
Crags, Edward, 23
Cranes, 35-36, 178
Crooms Hill, 40
Crossness Engines Museum, 71
Crowley, Ambrose, 28
Crown Lands, 18

Cruden, 104
Crystal Palace Exhibition, 193
Cutty Sark, 86, 88
Cutty Sark Pub, 28, 154
Cyclopean wall, 119
Davies, Anne, 150
Davies, Mike, 194
Davies, Thomas, 152
Dead Dog Bay, 34
Delta Metal, 108, 179, 180, 181, 187, 202
Denmark Hill, 76
Dent, Wilkinson, 79
Deptford Creek, 20, 62, 64
Derek Jarman style garden, 179
Derwent Street, 32, 72
Despatch, 85
Developes 26
Dick, Alexander, 179
Dining rooms, 188
Dock, 34, 95, 96, 97, 98, 99, 114, 163, 164, 165, 166
Docklands, 190, 191, 192, 200, 203
Docwra, 126, 127
Dog Kennel Field, 19, 29
Dolphin Yard Museum, 109
Dome, 6, 26, 81, 135, 136, 160, 162, 170, 193 -199, 202, 205
Dome of Discovery, 194
Donkin, Brian, 24, 69
Dorman Long, 178
Dr.Who, 133
Drainage system, 8
Drapers, 12
Dreadnought School, 189
Drew, William, 156, 158
Dry dock 81, 95, 97, 99, 126, 154
Dry Docks Corporation of London, 98
Dryden, Mr., 22
Dundonald, Earl of, 59
Dunkirk, 103, 109
Durham coalfield, 32, 33
Dyes, 66
East Greenwich Library, 171
East Greenwich No.1, 127, 128
East Greenwich Portland Cement Company, 115
East India Company, 13, 42, 82
East Lodge, 113, 148-153

Eastney Street, 18, 161
Easton & Anderson, 169
Eastwoods, 187
Ecology Centre, 109
Edmonds, Augustus, 105, 111
Elliot, George 43
Eliot, John, 23
Eliot, Lord, 23
Elizabethan, 101
Elswick Works, 76
Emirate's Airline, 199
Enderby Brothers, 11, 39, 67
Enderby family, 20
Enderby Group, 52, 201
Enderby House, 17, 42, 52, 53, 148, 160, 201
Enderby Land', 41
Enderby Wharf, 8, 16, 20, 38-51, 148, 155, 199, 201
Enderby, Charles, 40 - 42
Enderby, Samuel, 39
Engineers, 70, 72
Environment Agency, 204
Ernest Piper, 106
Exhauster, 69
Explosion, 24
Extruded Metals Co Ltd., 180
Faraday, Michael, 40
Farnborough, 30
Farrell, Terry, 172
Festival Hall, 179
Festival of Britain, 193
Fire, 18, 23, 33, 41, 67, 100, 115
Firework factory, 145
First flash', 75
Fishing'., 6
Fitzpatrick, Daniel, 84
Flavell's Mews, 72
Flax, 40
Footpath, 126
Forbes Abbott, 142
Fred, 109
Free crossings, 168
Fuel Research Institute, 135
Fullers brewery, 155, 160
#gas cookers, 68
Gas industry waste products, 54
Gas works, 37, 67, 69, 97, 99, 124-127, 130-136, 143, 144, 163, 174, 187, 190-195

Gatehouse, Blackwall Tunnel, 170
Ghent, 207
Ghost, 136
Ghost bus' 194
Gibbet, 20-21
Giralda, 105, 106, 109
Gladstone Cartridge Co., 147
Glass Elliot, 43- 46
Glass, Richard, 43, 49
Glemsford Silk Mill, 70
Glenforth Street, 146
Glenvilles, 183, 184
Glucose syrup, 183
Goldsmith's of Grays, 106
Golf range, 179
Gooch, Daniel, 45, 48, 49
Goose Marsh, 8
Goulburn Historic Waterworks Museum, 71
Grafton crane, 35
Grain neutral alcohol, 184
Granite Wharf, 7, 31, 118, 201
Gravel, 30
Grazing., 15
Great Eastern, 48, 49, 50
Great Globe, 118, 119
Great Meadow, 29, 32
Great Pitts, 55
Great War, 131, 173, 176, 180, 183, 185, 189
Greater London Council, 35, 172, 191
Greater London Industrial Archaeology Society, 175
Green Man Pub, 28
Greenwich and South Eastern Docks, 164
Greenwich Board of Works, 8
Greenwich Boys, 169
Greenwich Council, 185, 188, 190, -193, 204
Greenwich Inlaid Lino, 176
Greenwich Labour Party, 171
Greenwich Millennium Village, 197-199
Greenwich Power Station, 28
Greenwich Railway, 28
Greenwich South Street, 31
Greenwich Town Social Club, 159

Greenwich Waterfront Development Partnership, 184
Greenwich Wharf, 31-36
Greenwich Yacht Club, 109, 153
Gregory,, Olinthus 22
Greig & Co.'s Mills, 139
Greig's Wharf, 185, 187
Guano, 64, 143
Guardian newspaper, 136
Guided bus, 194
Gunpowder, 10, 17, 18, 218
Gunpowder Depot, 10, 26
Gurney Hanbury 156
Gutta Percha, 44, 45, 46
Gwynne's, Pumps 70
Haberdashers Company, 57
Hall, John, 24, 150
Halloween, 86, 88, 89
Hancock, Walter, 63
Hanson, 74, 177, 178, 187, 202
Harbour Master, 37, 161
Hardee, Malcolm, 158
Harris, Cllr Bob, 193
Harrison Barber, 173, 216
Hatcham Manor Farm, 57
Hatcliffe Charity, 12, 148
Haystack, 15
Heart's Content, 49, 51
Hemp, 38, 39, 40, 46
Henley, William Thomas, 45
Henry Rifled Barrel Engineering and Small Arms Co., 147
Henworth, 100
Hewes, Jamet, 151
High pressure steam, 23
Hills, Arnold, 62
Hills, Arthur, 56, 62
Hills, Edwin, 62
Hills, Frank, 61, 56, 61-68, 133, 148, 152
Hills, Thomas, 62
Hodges, Butler and Dale, 122
Holcombe, Charles, 43, 55-57, 104, 113-116, 141
Holiday Inn., 173
Hollick, Jabez, 34, 114
Hook , Alastair, 160
Horn Lane, 8
Horniman Museum, 190
Horse omnibus service, 15

HorseshoeBreach, 9, 58, 81-84, 113
Hounson, John, 38
House of Lords, 97
Housing, 10, 27-33
Howden, Gidley, 55
Hughan, Thomas, 101, 110
Hughes & Co, 111
Humphrey and Grey, 110
Hyam, Samuel, 97
Ice well, 34
Iddenden Cottages, 148, 184
IKEA, 190
Imperial Gas Company, 60
Imperial Stone, 122
Imperial Wharf, 122
Improved Wood Pavement Co. 59, 61
Interserve, 111, 187
Isle of Dogs, 6, 114, 126, 178
Jacubaits, Joe, 101
James Piper barge, 105, 106
Jetty, Delta, 181
Jetty, Greenwich Council, 44, 51, 53, 74, 117, 121, 127, 133, 174, 175, 179, 183, 186, 202
Jetty, power station, 175
John Earl of Chatham, 23
John Harrison Way, 135, 178
John Stewart & Sons, 99
John W. Mackay, 51
Johnson and Phillips, 174, 181
Johnson, Boris, 195
Johnson, William, 22, 150
Joyce, William, 64
Jubilee Line, 192, 194, 203
Kampultican, 175
Kao, Charles, 51
Kaptan Sukru, 91
Kaye, Joseph, 60
Kenny's jetty, 179
Kent, 7
Kentish Mercury, 31
King's Sluice, 8
Kirkcaldy, 177
Knackers, 173
Knight Dragon, 101, 109, 198, 201, 202
Kuper, William, 43
Kyan's sublimate, 40
Lady Derby, 84, 85, 89

Lambarde's Wall, 6
'Lambton Terrace', 33
Lawes, F.C., 64, 65
Lay Lines, 202
Lea Ness, 6
Lennard still, 142
Leonard Piper, 107
Lewis and Stockwell, 95
Lillie, John Scott, 116
Limekilns, 30
Linoleum, 75, 175, 176, 177
Littlewood, James, 38
Livesey Institute, 130
Livesey, George, 124-130, 136, 158
Lloyd and Ostell, 22
London and Regional, 36
London County Council, 8, 72, 94, 128, 148, 167, 168, 172, 186, 190
London Metal Exchange, 35
London Phosphate Syndicate, 122
London School Board School, 189
London Seed Crushing Co, 139
London Steel and Ordnance Co, 75
London Yacht Club', 151
Lovell House, 35
Lovell's Wharf, 31, 201
Low carbon energy centre, 198
Lubbock, Sir John, 29
Macaroni, Francis, 64, 68
Magazine, gunpowder, 17, 18, 68, 91,
Mahoney, Mary, 146
Maize, 183, 184
Manganese bronze, 74, 145
Marsh Lane, 8, 113, 114
Maudslay Son and Field, 84, 86, 92
Maudslay, Herbert, 85, 93
Maze Hill Station, 28, 31
Meantime Brewery, 160
Mechanic's Arms, 158
Memorial Park, 135
Mercers Company, 12, 13, , 28 54
Metropolitan Board of Works, 78, 128, 168
Metropolitan Borough of Greenwich, 185
Metropolitan Storage and Trade Co. Ltd, 178
Metropolitan Toll Bridges Act, 168

Michael Nairn, 176, 177
Millennium Dome, 21
Millennium Exhibition, 101, 197
Millington, 28
Mission to Seamen, 189
Mitre Pub, 158
Mockford 'Ordnance' Manure Works, 143
Molassine, 181, 182, 184
Moore, George, 20, 113
Morden Castle, 156
Morden College, 9-15, 26-38, 42-45, 54-62, 70, 75, 78-83, 93-95, 100-105, 108, 111, 116, 126, 141, 143-144, 148, 154-155, 163, 195, 201, 207- 208
Morden Wharf, 43-45, 55, 57, 113-115, 158, 202
Morden Wharf Road, 57
Morgan Stanley 1973 report, 192
Mowlem, John, 118, 119
Murch, Kaye, 135
Museum in Docklands, 99
Mystic Seaport, 83
Nailor, Thomas, 24
Nairns of Kirkaldy, 75
Naphtha, 40
National Benzole, 186
National Company for Boat Building by Machinery., 81
National grid, 174
Naval rope walk, 38
Naval tank vessels, 85
New Millennium Experience, 8, 153, 179, 195, 201
New Orleans, 101
Newall's of Gateshead, 43, 46
Newcastle, 62, 66, 74, 76, 97, 134
Non-ferrous metals, 35
North Greenwich Station, 194
Norton Excelsior, 171
Norton, Dick, 109
Norton's Yard, 109
O'Driscoll, Pat, 109
Old Court', 7
Opium War, 79
Optic cloak', 198
Ordnance Arms, 157
Ordnance Draw Dock, 101, 126, 169

Ordnance Tar Works 71, 79, 132, 142
Ordnance Wharf, 26, 54, 71, 78, 95, 100, 132, 142, 143, 202
Orinoco, 111, 213, 222
Paddock Place, 119
Paint, 57, 109, 176
Parsons, Percival, 72, 145
Pascoe and Wright, 97
Patent stone, 121
Pear Tree Marsh, 113
Peartree Way, 6, 199
Pelton Arms, 32
Pelton Main Colliery 32
Pelton Road, 27-33
Pemrose, Roger, 198
Pender, John, 45
Penn, John, 67
Phoenix Gas Company, 78
Phoenix Stone Works, 117
Phoenix Wharf, 132
Phosphor Bronze Company, 180
Pilot, 10, 21-23, 113, 129, 135, 149, 150, 178
Piper, James, 105
Piper's, 31, 105, 106, 107, 109, 201
Pitt, William, 23
Pitts, 8
Plummer, Desmond, 172
Podd's Elms Reach, 21
Point Wharf, 101, 110, 173, 202
Pollution, 188, 199, 205
Poor of Farningham, 12
Port of London Authority, 99, 162, 185
Portland cement works, 114
Price, Lewis, 20
Primrose Pier, 183
Prince of Wales, 93, 94
Profit sharing, 128, 129
Propeller, 68
Providence Wharf, 31, 111, 185
Pubs, 154
Pukwana, Dudu, 158
Purification, gas 65
Quantum Cloud, 133, 195
Railway locomotives, 70
Ransome, Frederick, 121, 149
Ransome Concrete Co., 122
Ransome, Ernest Leslie, 121, 122

Ranworth 157
Ravenhill, and Salkeld, 96
Ravensbourne College, 198
Redpath Brown, 153, 178, 179, 195
Reid, Henry, 113, 115, 116
Rennie, John 9
Rheocrete Paving Stone Slab Co, 122
Richmond Hill, 98
Rifled ordnance, 76
Rito,, 182
Riverside Gardens, 7, 36, 145, 192, 201
Riverside footpath, 95, 204
Riverside Steel Works', 179
Riverside tram, 194
Riverway, 8, 149, 150, 153
Roberts, Bob, 103
Robson, Thomas, 145
Roman Cement, 113, 115
Romans, 6
Rope, 38, 39, 40, 41, 43
Roper family, 12
Roque's map, 12
Rotary steam engine, 67, 69
Rothbury Hall, 80, 189
Rowton, Frederick, 33
Royal Arsenal, 16, 73, 74, 76
Royal Docks, 101, 199
Royal Dockyard, 41
Royal Geographical Society, 40
Royal Magazine, 18
Rumenco, 183
Rural industry, 15
Russell, George, 22, 23, 113, 150,
Safeguarded wharves, 192
Sahilbent, 90, 91
Sailing barges, 81, 102, 105, 106, 107, 109
Salomans, David, 164, 168
Salution' house, 154, 155
Samuda Brothers, 95
Science Museum, 75
Screw collier, 84
Sea coal, 37, 161
Sea wall, 9
Sea Witch, 57, 104, 156, 157
Second World War, 99, 107, 109, 116, 122, 134, 136, 159, 169-185, 189, 190

Sharpe and Handasyde, 24
Sharpe, Philip, 22, 113
Shaw Lovell, 35
Ship repair, 96, 97
Shipbuilding, 81, 92
Shoddy, 64, 144
Shooters Hill, 68
Shrubsall, Horace, 108
Silos, 184, 185
Silvertown TNT explosion, 127
Silvertown Tunnel, 172, 182, 199
Sirket-I-Hayriye, 90, 91
Skylon, 194
Slice of Reality, 195
Smell, 64, 65, 126
Smith, George, 13, 26-32, 54-55, 58
Smoke elimination process, 135
Soames, James, 104, 140, 141
Soap, 22, 104, 140, 141, 174, 183
Soar Mill Cove, 89
South Eastern Railway, 163-166, 194
South Metropolitan Electricity Company, 174
South Metropolitan Gas, 26, 69, 79, 97, 98, 124, 128, 135, 143, 158, 166, 213
Spain, 62, 66
Spent oxide, 103
Spinnaker sail, 93
SS Persian, 44
St Andrews, 189
St.John's Park, 122
St.John's railway disaster, 179
St.Peter's Abbey, 7
Staines, 115, 116, 176
Staircase access to Blackwall Tunnel, 169
Standard Ammonia Co., 142
Star in the East, 74, 121, 157
Steam road vehicle, 63, s68
Steam Traps, 72
Steel works, 73, 74, 75, 76, 79
Stein, Arthur, 182
Stephenson, George, 68
Stockholm tar, 54
Stockwell and Lewis, 95, 97, 143
Stones of Deptford, 89
Street lighting, 40
Submarine telegraph cable, 43

Suhulet, 90, 91
Sulphate store, 133
Sulphuric acid, 20, 62, 64, 66, 144
Superphosphate, 65, 143
Sussex Wharf,, 142
Swanage, 118, 119
Swiss bitumen, 54
Syral,, 185
Tar, 55, 67, 103
Tasmania, 96
Tate and Lyle, 182, 184
Taylor, Thomas, 22, 113, 150
Telegraph Construction and Maintenance Co, 45-49, 192
Telegraph Hill, 128
Tereos, 185
Thames Church Mission., 150
Thames Conservators, 74
Thames Craft., 110
Thames Foundry, 72
Thames Iron Works, 169
Thames Soap Works, 140, 141
Thames Steam Soap Works, 141
Thamescraft Dry Docking, 101
The North and South Metropolitan Junction Railway, 164
Thermalloys, 183
Thompson, Nathan, 81, 82, 83, 84
Thorne, Will, 128, 130
Thornley Street, 32
Tickner, Thomas, 113
Tide mill, 7, 22, 62, 64, 113, 148, 150, 173, 174, 195
Tilbury Contracting and Dredging, 111, 187
Tilling horse bus, 171
Times, 62
Track ways, 6
Trade unions, 128, 129
Trafalgar Road, 67
Tram route, 30, 166
Tram telephone box, 167
Tramatorium, 166
Travers Morgan, 191
Travers' map, 27
Treaty of Amiens, 23
Trevithick, Richard, 23-24
Trinity Hospital, 12, 28, 100
Trinity House, 9
Tudor Palace, 16

Tugs, 85
Tunnel Avenue, 146, 167, 170, 171, 185, 188, 191
Tunnel Avenue Depot, 185
Tunnel Club, 158
Tunnel Refineries, 183
Turkey, 90, 92
Tysoe, Joseph, 127
Union Tavern, 28, 154
Union Wharf, 154
United Lamp Black Works, 188
United Ship Builders & Repairers, 185
Urban Aid, 191
Usta, Mehmed, 90
V1 hit, 159
Valentia, 46, 48, 49, 51
Valentine's House, 57
Vansittart, Henry, 18
Vavasseur, Josiah, 80, 189
Ventilation shafts, 169
Vickers, Son and Maxim, 71
Victoria Deep Water Terminal., 177-178, 202
Victoria Wharf, 70, 74, 121, 176, 177
Vims dog biscuits, 182
Vitriol, 20
Waddell and Co, 34
Waldridge, 32
Wallscot, 8, 9
Wallsend coal, 34
Wally Butcher and the Laughing Gravy Orchestra., 158
Walton, Frederick, 75, 121, 175

War Memorial, 130, 135
Warwick Cottages, 114
Watch house, 10
Watkins Tugs, 70
Weguelin, Christopher, 143
West Ham Football Club, 62
West India Dock, 9, 10
West, James, 104
Westcombe Park Road, 33
Westcombe Park Station, 129
Whaling ships, 40
Wheatley, 15
Whitbread's Brewery, 156
Whiteway's Wharf, 33
Whitworth Street, 32
Wilkie and Soames, 140, 141
Williams the Pirate, 21
Williams, Richard Price, 74
Willis and Wright, 58, 87, 88, 117
Willis, John, 86
Willow Dyke, 30
Wilson, Reginald P., 174
Winkfield Bell, 113
Wood preservative, 54
Wooden nutmeg, 82
Woodlands, 162
Woolwich and South East London Tramways Company, 167
Woolwich Road, 6, 8
Woolwich's Public Hall, 84
Wylam Fuel Co, 144
Xylonite, 104
Yarmouth Carriers, 35
Young, Mr, 39
Young's, 154, 160

232

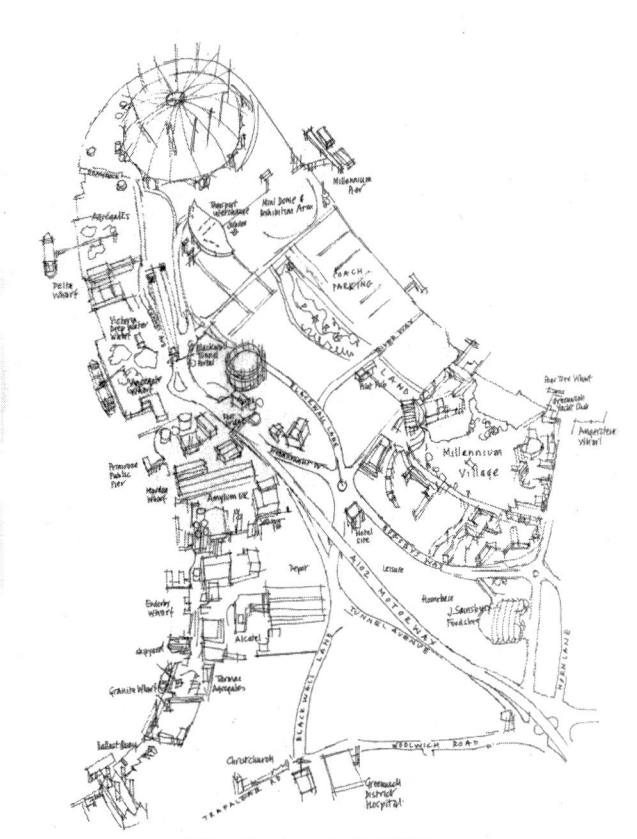

The Peninsula in 2000
Drawing thanks to Peter Kent

Printed in Great Britain
by Amazon